HITCHHIKING FOR UGLY PEOPLE

PETER FITZSIMONS

HITCHHIKING FOR UGLY PEOPLE

*...and
other life
experiences*

RANDOM HOUSE
AUSTRALIA

Random House Australia Pty Ltd
20 Alfred Street, Milsons Point, NSW 2061

Sydney New York Toronto
London Auckland Johannesburg
and agencies throughout the world

First published 1994

National Library of Australia
Cataloguing-in-Publication Data

FitzSimons, Peter.
  Hitchhiking for ugly people.

  ISBN 0 09 182967 4.

  i. FitzSimons, Peter - Anecdotes. 2. FitzSimons, Peter -
Humor. 3. Australian wit and humor. I. Title.

A828.303

Typeset in 10/12 Meridien by Midland Typesetters, Victoria
Printed by Griffin Paperbacks, Adelaide
Production by Vantage Graphics, Sydney

Dedication

To my late mother, Helen FitzSimons O.A.M., who never once failed to pick me up when driving past. She was a wonderful woman.

Acknowledgements

I should like to warmly thank both the *Sydney Morning Herald* and the London *Daily Telegraph* for their kindness in allowing me to reprint in this book some of the pieces first published in their pages. I should also like to thank Allen & Unwin Australia for permission to reprint some of the very best of the pieces from *Basking in Beirut*, and Mike Oliver for the fine illustration on the front cover.

Thanks too, to my publisher Matthew Kelly, whose advice was invaluable and whose deadlines were once again commendably malleable. Also to Henry Barrkman for his skilled work on the manuscript.

Finally, my warm thanks to my wife Lisa, for reading it all ten times through and giving me wonderful support throughout.

Contents

The Holiday House

'EVERY HOUR, EVERY DAY, every week, every year you spend in a place, you take some of it away with you and you leave part of yourself there.'
Guy de Maupassant

The house came to us after Grandpa died. 'Nantucket' it was called—at Newport, on Sydney's northern peninsula. From the year dot, our family had moved into the old house for a week over summer, and Grandpa would rent it out for the rest of the time. But now that Mum and Dad were the new land-lords, they figured we might as well move in for as long as ten days, and damn the expense.

Nantucket had been built by Grandpa back in 1923, when Newport was little more than a few houses in some scattered cow paddocks. Back then, the trip to get there from the family home in Wahroonga involved about an hour's drive down the dirt track that was Mona Vale Road and, so the family legend goes, the kidney-rattler used to always pass cars that had boiled over going up Tumbledown Dick Hill.

For us Fitzes, though, the trip to Newport from our farm at Peats Ridge was not the time-consuming part—it was the day preceding it that would sap us white. Dad wouldn't leave the tomatoes till they were completely picked and weeded, Mum wouldn't leave the house till it looked like it was part of a Hoover showroom, and we six kids were their faithful Trojans. Usually, our target time of departure was five pm on Christmas Eve, and we'd leave about nine o'clock, when Mum and Dad could stand our whingeing no more. (I suppose I was about seven when I discovered the way to *really* get to them was to sit in the stationwagon from about eight pm onwards and beep the horn till their noses bled.)

So we'd eventually leave—the back towbar carving a small groove down our dirt track, so heavily were we loaded—through air thick with the smell of newly irrigated soil. Dad would habitually empty half the dam onto the oranges and tomatoes in an effort to get them through the next few days without him.

When we got to Nantucket a couple of hours later, the doors would spring open and disgorge all of us, racing up the stairs to 'bags' our beds. Ah, sea air, and that marvellous thump-thump-thump of the waves hitting the beach about one hundred metres down the hill.

It was the swimming in the sea that really got to us. *Looxury!* Back on the farm, the general rule was that Dad would take us all swimming down at the dam only after we'd filled a trailer full of stones from the top cow paddock. It was hard yakka, even if it made the swim more enjoyable when it eventually came. But down at Nantucket, the basic gist was—unless you were still a littlie—all you had to do for a swim was to look-left-and-then-right-and-then-left-again, and then remember to keep between the flags.

If you were still a littlie, though, the scheme was somewhat different. Then you had to stick very close to Mum or Dad or one of your big brothers or sisters and—with their eyes upon you—act as if you would surely die if the water touched your heels. Screaming and laughing all the way, you'd run back and forth like a loon, up and down the sandbank in front of every breaking and receding wave. I know it can't be true, but the memory that is implanted in my brain from my days as a three year old is running back and forth, up and down the beach, as one after another of these *Poseidon Adventure* tidal waves threatened to engulf me.

Our folks would never lose sight of us, even on the busiest of beach days . . . for not only were we their own beloved flesh and blood, but they also knew we were the only kids on the beach wearing those wretched big yellow life jackets. See, for them, the loose city ways could garn get knotted—it was the safety code of the country dam that still applied for their kids and that was that. Lifesavers or no lifesavers.

With that wonderful tight-skinned feeling of being almost sunburnt, we'd then go up to Nantucket for a lunch, invariably of Christmas leftovers and a bit of salad, and then back to the beach. At least, we kids would go back to the beach.

But rarely Dad. It was a cause of quite some family mirth that after working fifty-one weeks a year, hard physical labour on the farm, Dad still wouldn't be able to relax enough when he was at Nantucket to get away from work. While the rest of us would go to the beach, play endless games of cards, Monopoly and charades, Dad would be fixing fences, painting walls and hammering doors back on to their hinges while Mum would be mostly in the kitchen.

As a break from this, Mum and Dad would usually go back home to the farm one day of the holiday week—to pick the tomatoes, irrigate the oranges or somesuch—and we kids would stay down, troubled perhaps a fraction that under the same hot sun we, their children, would be on the beach, while they were on their knees on the farm. But, hey, you get over it, you know?

When Dad had his heart attack back in 1979, right there at the kitchen table at Nantucket on Boxing Day, it was awful. We took him into the bedroom and laid him down on the bed and I shall never forget the terrible realisation I had then, that he was actually mortal. That's a long time ago, now, and he's fine.

He'll be down at Nantucket with the rest of us this summer. With a lot of family additions from the last ten years. For the tribe is getting bigger now. The third generation, which took so long to get started, has now taken a firm hold and is consolidating its position all the time, moving out of their early infant trenches and forging ahead. They've got a way to go yet before they completely overrun us—but already there are signs that they will eventually come for us.

Personally, I'll be waiting. With a baseball bat if I have to. Crunch time will come when one of my nephews figures he has the right to the last slice of apple pie before me. It will get very very ugly then, and I'll have to be a very, very old man before I give in on that one.

But I hope I'm still at Nantucket.

Mrs Hammond

IT WAS ONE of those scenes that was quite normal for us Fitzes, but so staggering to visitors that on more than one occasion they simply dropped their cups of tea outright.

Our whole family would be out on our sunny terrace having morning tea with whichever one of Mum or Dad's old school friends had chanced to drop by our farm at Peat's Ridge on their way through to Sydney. And our cleaning lady, Mrs Hammond, would be busily sweeping up outside the backdoor when it would happen . . . Mrs Hammond would suddenly look up and yell: 'These F---ING Fitty's and their BLOODY toffee-nosed FRIENDS think they're so BLOODY GOOD!, but they're all just a pack of SHITS!'

And Mum would just continue pouring the tea and making polite conversation as if nothing had happened—which to her mind was the case—while the visitors would sit, struck dumb, vainly trying to pick up the thread of their previous thoughts. They might just have got themselves together enough for one of them to come back with a rejoinder to Mum of 'Yes, uh,

Helen, it will be a relief if the southerly buster hits this, er . . . afternoon', while still looking nervously over at Mrs Hammond's furious sweeping, when it would happen again: 'SLUTS!' Mrs Hammond would erupt. 'BASTARDS! Dropping in HERE like LORD and LADY F---ING MUCK and expecting the BLOODY Fitty's to drop all their FRIGGING farmwork, and I WON'T STAND FOR IT.'

The visitors would then look around at the rest of us kids, or at Dad, for confirmation that something seriously weird was going on, but always with the same result—nothing, nothing at all.

In absolute truth, most often we would quite genuinely have failed to notice that anything at all was out of the ordinary. For us six kids, Mrs Hammond's constant swearing was the soundtrack that had been playing in the background ever since we'd been born. As a result, we'd long before ceased to hear what she was actually saying any more than we focused on the individual sounds of the cries of passing kookaburras.

Mrs Hammond was just a bit 'touched', that was all, and it was no big deal. If we ever did ask our parents about it, Mum would say that Mrs Hammond wasn't nasty herself, it was just that the voices she was hearing were nasty and we shouldn't pay any attention.

'There are all types in the world,' she said, 'and you've just got to try and get along with them all the best you can.' Which was good enough for us. More scones?

She was a woman of singular appearance, was our Mrs Hammond. No more than a couple of feet taller than the doorhandle, but strong enough to break the door down if she needed to, she had shoulders that were somehow out of all proportion to the rest of her body, and still that wasn't the oddest thing. For a reason I could never quite fathom, if she didn't shave at least every four or five days we would see the beginnings of a small beard start to grow.

My main memory, though, is of her thick curly grey hair, equally thick glasses, and an expression that alternated between inner amusement and outward rage. It all depended on what the demons inside her head were saying to her . . .

Those demons had been there a long time, I guess. She'd

spent something like fifteen years in a psychiatric hospital at Gladesville, and had only been discharged from there because the hospital authorities had found it impossible to cope with her boundless energy.

Apparently, an independent government authority had done a study of the asylum and been appalled to find that one of the inmates, our very own Mrs Hammond, was running the whole show. It was she who made the porridge, did the laundry and watered the garden, all before breakfast, and from then on she simply didn't stop, going like a work-tornado through the whole day. The report said it was simply inadmissible for an inmate to be so pivotal to the functioning of the place, and after she'd been obliged to leave, the real staff reluctantly had to go back to work.

Soon after she'd come out of the asylum, probably at the age of fifty or so, she'd looked around for accommodation somewhere close to her son, a bloke who lived a couple of miles away from us, and that's how she came into our lives.

After an approach from her son, Mum and Dad said she could live in what we called 'the flat'—some fairly basic accommodation that we had at the back of our old green shed. As soon as they'd confirmed that, despite her vitriolic expostulations, Mrs Hammond wasn't actually dangerous they'd begun to employ her, at first bit by bit, and then on a more regular basis.

She was useful around the house, as Mum would often be completely flattened under the myriad household chores involved in getting six kids clothed, fed and off to school. With one hand, Mrs Hammond could brush Trish's long hair straight and beautiful in about thirty seconds flat, so vigorously did she brush; with the other she would be ironing one of my school shirts, while at the same time kicking my brother Jum's school satchel over to him from under the chair where he always left it. She swore most of the time, but with occasional bursts of lucidity, in which we really could converse with her quite normally.

I think the real Mrs Hammond had quite a lot of affection for Mum and Dad for giving her an honest wage and a place to live—it was just the voices she heard really did say very nasty things and when she was on the air it was those voices which held sway.

Not that we were the only ones who copped it. If the voices ever gave us a leave pass from being insulted, they would usually give a terrible workover to one 'Mrs Todd', who some twenty years earlier had borrowed a pound of butter and made the serious mistake of never returning it. Little did Mrs Todd know that that error would see her name constantly bursting forth on blue airwaves for the next four decades or so . . .

Despite it all, somehow or other we liked her a lot. There was an inner kindness in there somewhere which we could just discern through filthy mutterings and she was for a long time a part of the fabric of our lives. If Mum was on top of things and didn't need her quite so badly, it was in helping Dad with the farmwork that Mrs Hammond was really outstanding.

In those days it was said that a good man who really bent his back should be able to pick ten bushels of peas in a day. Mrs Hammond would habitually pick fifteen bushels. Actually, she wouldn't so much 'pick' the peas, as pursue a personal vendetta against them, raging at each and every one that had had the temerity to stay on the vine instead of jumping voluntarily into her bucket. Muttering all the while, she would hurl the peas into her bucket with the glee of one who knew all along she'd get the little buggers in the end, and it bloody well served them right.

And all day long she'd go. Dad would make her stop for lunch and tea, but I really think if left to her own devices she would have just kept on into the night.

When the day was done, and Dad would say it was time to 'knock off', she would return to the flat to do whatever it was she did there. Whatever it was, it still involved a lot of loud cursing. At night, even though she was a good three hundred yards away, when we kids would go out on to our verandah to sleep we could still hear her voice wafting to us on the breeze:

F---ING FITZSIMONS's! . . . MONGREL KIDS! . . . SNOTTY-NOSED LITTLE BRATS! BLOODY . . . BASTARDS!

And so on. As often as not, Mrs Hammond's insults would be

the last thing I would hear as I would drift off to sleep . . .

Even all these years on, whenever I am having difficulty nodding off, I always wonder whether I should wake Lisa beside me and ask her to go about three hundred metres down the road and start yelling obscene imprecations into the wind at the top of her voice.

I'm sure I'd be asleep in no time at all.

The Cave

ONE BY ONE, they left us.

David, as the oldest brother, was first. Off to the big city, to 'boarding school', whatever that was. By the time I was six years old, brother Andrew and sister Cathy had also up and left the farm. Even my brother Jum left us in the end—taken by Mum in the stationwagon one fine February morning. I remember him waving goodbye as he left, with the maddeningly superior air of one who feels he has just crossed the portals of adulthood.

But the hell with it. My sister Trish and I didn't care. Not one little bit.

Let him go. Let them *all* go off to their big-city ways. We had no doubt that Jum would come back in the school holidays with the usual stories of buildings bigger than pine trees and so many cars on the road you couldn't keep count. Sure, he'd try and impress us with all the fancy-pants things he'd learnt— *Bonjour, comment allez-vous?* etc—but who needed all that nonsense, anyway?

Not my sister and me. Trish and I kept on at Peat's Ridge

Primary School regardless. We were proud that despite the defections of our older siblings, we had remained entirely loyal to the country life, staying with Mum and Dad and the orchard through thick and thin.

In contrast to the newly soft ways of our four older brothers and sister (who, we knew, were watching televisions, drinking Coca-Colas and doing all sorts of other weak and disloyal things), we were *tough*, see? Damn right, we were. Not only did we still not know the difference between a TV set and a ham sandwich, but we had *no intention* of finding out. In the meantime we helped Dad fight bushfires, rounded up some of the cattle on our own, climbed trees and went for long walks down the valley into the huge area of thick scrub that surrounded the farm. We'd *never* go soft like them, we vowed. Never, ever. Whatever happened.

It nearly killed me when Trish went to the Big Smoke too. Just like the others, suddenly dressed in a strange uniform and leaving me behind in the stationwagon dust as Mum drove her out between the palm trees. But at least good ol' Trish had *promised* she wouldn't change, swore blind that she'd stay true, and I took her at her word.

For myself, even if I had a keen sense of the responsibility of now being the last one left standing, still I couldn't wait for her to come back in the school holidays to see if she'd kept her promise.

She had. So much so that when she showed up again in May with all the others she could barely wait to tell me of her 'plan', whereby we could prove to each other how tough we two still were.

What we are going to do Petey-boy, she told me, was 'go down the valley and spend the night camping in The Cave!'

'. . . .'

It wasn't that I didn't *want* to spend a whole night in The Cave, just on our own, out there with all the wild animals, without Mum or Dad nearby or anything—in fact I could think of nothing I'd rather do more to show how tough we were—but I was *sure* that Dad wouldn't let us, so there's really no point in even asking . . .

Dad thought it was a great idea. From the moment Jum

had piped up and said he knew exactly which cave we meant and he could take Dad there at a moment's notice if he wanted to check on us, our father was right behind the project

Good ol' Jum.

Even then the whole thing might not have been a goer if it weren't for the chocolate crackles. Sensing perhaps a remaining reluctance on my part, Trish had baked a whole batch of chocolate crackles and promised that we could have them for dessert on our adventure that night. Otherwise she wouldn't give me any at all. Then came the killer: 'What are you, a scaredy-cat?'

We made ready a couple of hours before sundown. A sleeping bag each, a couple of chops and sausages Mum had packed for us, some matches replete with instructions to 'only light the campfire and nothing else', and, of course, the chocolate crackles. Dad was working down on the tomatoes when we left, but Mum gave us a hug and told us to look after each other, and so there was now nothing for it but to go. Even Trish could see that in the end. There was only one way to proceed, and that way led east from the farmhouse, down the hill, and down to the valley below—down to The Cave. We had to take it.

It had been a dry year as I recall. Hughie had not been busy. I say 'Hughie', because often if we were in a dry spell and there would be some rain, Mum and Dad would charge out into it and yell up at the skies, 'Send 'er down, Hughie!' all the while waving their arms around. They didn't really mean it or anything, like it was an actual raindance, but it never hurt either—and it always seemed to me the rain fell a bit heavier after they did it.

That night Hughie outdid himself. The rain came probably about an hour after sunset, teeming down, just as Trish and I were lying there feeling like sick bandicoots after so many chocolate crackles and burnt chops. It was a biting, horrible rain that stung the skin whenever a strong gust of wind would drive it in at us, which was often.

In truth, our 'cave' was more of a rock overhang that provided only scant protection against such a storm. Still, how glad we were that we were out here in the elements rather than back in soft warm beds like our four weak older brothers and sisters back at the farmhouse. We wouldn't change places with them for *quids*.

Then we heard it. An engine in the distance. Getting closer, then fading away . . . close and then fading, again and again. On one of the close runs, we could see headlights, too, bouncing through the trees.

I didn't like to say anything to Trish for fear of frightening her—though I at least grabbed hold of her hand and squeezed it just to comfort her—but what I really wanted to know was just how many of them were there? Down in this valley, where normally a truck didn't pass from one year to the next, it was obvious to me that if we were hearing engines on this night of all nights, then it was because some very very bad men were out there looking for us, wanting to do us harm.

I didn't know why they wanted to, and I didn't care to speculate. But that there were at least half a dozen of them looking for us, I was morally certain. Well, let them. They'd have a lot of horrible hours ahead of them in this weather, if they wanted to find us in *this* cave. I wouldn't be at all surprised if Trish and I were the only two on the planet that knew about it, Jum's claims to Dad notwithstanding.

The sound of engines seemed to go for hours through the storm and though I eventually drifted off to sleep, the sound was still there in the near distance when I awoke cold and stiff a while later.

If only the dawn would come. I strained my eyes through the pitch black, looking for the barest sign of light on the horizon, but still nothing. I guess Hughie was still too busy with sending 'er down, to worry about sending the dawn, too, but it had to be close, I was sure of that.

I knew Trish was as wide awake as I was, the way you know these things without anything being said; but neither of us wanted to acknowledge our being awake. The first to speak would have shown terrible weakness.

The dawn, the dawn, the dawn, where was it? It had to be at least five in the morning I knew, so why couldn't we see even a hint of the new day? Finally, I could stand it no more and, weakness or no, jumped out of my wet sleeping bag and scrabbled around in the knapsack for a big clock that Mum, however bizarre, had included with our provisions. When I struck a match to see the time, I first saw Trish's eyes, peering out from her sleeping bag; she was as cold as a newt, and as interested to know the time as me. Together, we stared with horror at the clock face. Ten-thirty pm—we'd been in the cave a mere three and a half hours. Hughie played on. I got back into my bag, only three words escaping my lips, by now surely blue.

'Good night, Trish.'

'Good night, Petey-boy.'

It seemed like a year and a hundred nightmares and just the odd bit of sleep later before we finally saw the first genuine light of dawn. Then we heard the voice, clear as a bell and getting closer.

'*Triiiiiiiiiiishhh . . .! Peeeeeeete . . .! Cooo-eeeee!*'

It was our father's voice.

'*Daddddy!*' we yelled back as one voice, momentarily forgetting that now we were grown-ups we just called him 'Dad'. 'Over here!!!!'

I can still remember, in every detail, Dad kind of jog-trotting down the hill in his big Wellington rubber boots, with big hugs for both of us when he got to us.

As we walked back to the farm, he told us the story.

Nearing sunset last night, he'd knocked off work and decided it would be a good idea for Jum to take him to our cave to check we were all right. Jum took him to a cave all right, but it was the wrong one. So Dad had got worried and, in the middle of the storm, he had spent the next couple of hours driving the tractor up and down every track in the valley, looking for us. All to no avail, so, reluctantly, he'd quit. After sleeping badly, he'd set off on foot just before first light the following morning, looking for us some more and calling our names all the way.

That was very nice 'n' all, Dad, but there really had been no need; we'd been fine, we assured him.

When we got back for a hearty breakfast, Mum wanted to know had we passed a comfortable night?

Comfortable? *Of course* it wasn't comfortable, Mum. It was so cold our eyebrows had almost fallen off, the ground had been harder 'n hell, the food gritty as a clod of earth, and the wind so strong we'd seen a passing wombat holding onto a tree with both paws for fear of getting blown away. It was a *horrible* night, Mum.

Which is why we loved it so. For we were *tough*.

Dad

DAD DIED YESTERDAY. They took him away in the dusk.

In a little dark van, edging slowly down the row of orange trees he'd planted thirty years earlier, past the house he'd built with Mum, past the tennis court he'd carved out of the bush, between the two palm trees he'd planted at the entrance to the farm he'd named Windhill, then back down the dirt track he'd first ventured up forty-five years earlier.

When Mum and Dad bought the place soon after getting back from the war, Mum in New Guinea and Dad at El Alamein, it was little more than a roughly cleared patch of ground lying in thirty hectares of bushland up at Peat's Ridge. It came with a horse that Mum and Dad eventually tracked down to a lost paddock in the nearby State forest.

'Laddie' used to drag posts on a slide down to the passionfruit patch for them, and despite his aged lethargy, they reckoned him to be most intelligent, for a horse. If there were up to fourteen posts on the slide Laddie would pull OK, but he would refuse to budge if Dad put on so much as a splinter more.

When Mum and Dad finally lashed out on a tractor, Laddie was in his hay. At last he could watch contentedly from the side-lines as Mum steered the tractor up the row, her first child on her knee. Dad walked behind, steering the plough they'd found in the shed next to the two-room shack they lived in.

After the first crop of tomatoes were planted in their second season there, Dad would disappear at dawn each day and come back for a quick breakfast before going out again. He wasn't a frenetic worker—like McGrath up the road, who they reckoned would have three clods of earth in the air at once when digging a ditch—but Dad had amazing endurance and worked all day long. When Mum and Dad sent their first crop of tomatoes to the Sydney markets, they were almost speechless with pride.

These tomatoes were really no bigger than large strawberries, but the important thing was that they had been grown with their own hands, watered with the sweat off their own brow.

By the time I arrived on the scene thirteen years and six children later, things had sorted themselves out a bit. They had cleared much of the ground and built a new house on the property. The orange trees had been planted and a packing shed erected to help sort out the ever-growing crop of tomatoes.

I grew up in that packing shed. In the summer we would sit in there with Mum and Dad, packing the tomatoes late into the night. As the youngest, it was my job to paste on the labels proudly bearing Dad's name.

To keep us from getting bored, Dad would teach us poetry, the same poetry he'd learnt to keep his mind active during long nights by an anti-aircraft gun in Africa during the Second World War. He'd try to teach us a new stanza every night, which we would then recite at the end of those we had already learnt.

'Have another go, sonno.'

Yes, Dad . . .

'And Clancy of the Overflow came down to lend a hand.
No finer horseman ever held the reins,
For never a horse could throw him while the saddle-girths would
stand,

He learnt to ride while droving in the rain.'

Whereupon Dad would break in to say: 'On the plain, sonno, he learnt to ride while droving on the plain. Try it again.'

Somewhere in the packing shed would be our pet diamond snake, Kaa. We kids had found it one day in the garden and Dad had seconded it for a tour of duty in the packing shed to keep down the mice population. After two months, Dad figured Kaa had done the job and decided to let him go down in the State forest. So he put him in a sack, took him down the forest and let him slither away.

But like the homing pigeon we figured he must have swallowed some time in his past, Kaa kept slithering back to the warm and comfortable shed. Dad kept taking him further and further into the forest, and Kaa kept returning.

But one day, after we'd released him for the fourth time, Dad was slashing the thick grass in the top row of orange trees, and suddenly there were souvenir bits of Kaa *everywhere*.

Rain, which is so often the bane of many people's summers, was a hoped-for event with us. Dad loved it because it meant more tomatoes and oranges; we loved it because of divine providence, which deemed it unsound practice to pick either oranges or tomatoes when they were wet. After a really good rain, my brother Jum and I used to find a particularly large puddle and have sensational mud fights.

With so many children, things weren't easy for Mum and Dad financially, but they were helped immeasurably by the fact that we could eat so much of what we grew—oranges for breakfast, for lunch, for afternoon tea.

Milk for the table came from the family cow, Penny, whom Dad would milk every morning at the start of the workday. Tomatoes also formed a large part of our summer diet, and what we didn't eat, Mum bottled in an enormous Fowler's Vacola saucepan. During school holidays we picked these tomatoes as well as packed them, and the constant refrain in the background seemed always to be Alan McGilvray calling the cricket on the ABC.

There was only one radio, a battered trannie held together with wire, insulating tape and prayer. It invariably stayed with Dad. So you might be picking away in one row when Dad's head would pop up from another row with the news that 'Lillee's got another one!' and we would all break from picking for a while to gather round Dad for the details.

When Lillee and Thommo were at their height back in the summer of '76, we sometimes seemed to do more listening to cricket than picking tomatoes, but Dad didn't mind. After all, we had a genuine cricketing celebrity in our midst . . .

One of the casual workers, George Frost, had a big dent in his temple, which George told us he got when Sir Donald Bradman had hit a ball for what would have been a thundering four runs . . . except it had hit him in the head and left a permanent dip in his brow. Dad never told us any different, so we thought it must be so, and treated ol' George as something of an expert, often asking his opinion on all sorts of cricketing matters.

Not that it was all work, though.

At the end of the day, when Mr McGilvray would announce, 'And that is stumps for the day', we would generally take that as the signal for our own retirement from the field, and we'd go up to the house to play doubles tennis.

Back in the mid-sixties Dad and my older brothers had fashioned a clay court out of soil they'd laboriously brought by the trailer-load from the irrigation dam, and as a family we spent many happy hours on it. When I was twelve and Dad was fifty-eight, I'd most often be paired with him because it was a good balance to have the weakest player with the strongest. When Dad got older and I got stronger, we played together again, for exactly the same reason, yet Dad could still place the ball anywhere he wanted.

But they took him away in the dusk.

'Try it again sonno, you'll get it this time.'

Yes, Dad . . .

'Happy the man whose wish and care,
A few paternal acres bound,
Content to breathe his native air
In his own ground.'

American Football

ABOUT 150 MOONS AGO, as an exchange student in America after leaving Knox Grammar boarding school, I was the offensive tackle on the Finlay High School football team in Finlay, Ohio.

It may have been only high school sport, but being football and being American, the commitment to winning was so total I was obliged to work harder than I ever have, before or since. With eyeballs rolling in loud enthusiasm, we lifted weights, slashed sprints and smashed into each other under the discerning eye of the coaches ('Got to get your shoulder right on his knee, Peeete!').

With the cheerleaders 'Pepper Club', brass band, 'Pep Rallies' and constant team chants of 'We are Number One!' as a back-up to hours of training, playing, studying playsheets and watching game videos, it was nothing if not an education in this all-American game.

The games were played on a Friday night in front of a minimum of ten thousand screaming small-town fans with big-time ambitions for us. And being a member of the football team gave us as many strutting rights on the town streets as it did in the school.

But I never touched the leather. From the beginning of the long season to the very end, I never once got my hand on the ball during a game. Not even a sniff. As I remember it, when it came time for the end-of-season photo and I got to hold the ball on my knees in the middle of the front row, I was quite surprised at how light the damn thing was. No kidding.

And therein lies the problem with the whole game, at least from a player's perspective. While it may indeed provide a wonderful spectacle for those well enough steeped in the game to understand what on earth is going on, the bottom line is that in American football the efforts of ninety-five per cent of the players are directed exclusively to making the other five per cent shine, without ever getting a chance themselves.

Which, of course, is quite a contrast to the codes of American football's cousin. My theory is that if you were to put both rugby and rugby league into a pot and boil them right down till you got to the quintessential joys of each, you would be left with two identical gold ingots: the joy of running with the ball in your hands.

This joy does exist in American football—together with the added joy of throwing the ball long distances and catching it—but it's only the precious few that get to do it.

To be fair, this was only a problem for *me*, as I had known what it was to play another game where I was actually allowed to run with the ball. It presented less of a problem for my fellow frontline men who had never aspired to something so gloriously other-worldly as running or scoring, and were content to spend their time smashing opposing unfortunates for the greater good of the scoring players. At my school, we frontliners gave ourselves the apt title of Hogs. As a Hog, I had to content myself with making spaces for the fullback to run through, and, above all, to protecting the quarterback.

While the rest of us had an individual specialist coach always pumping us full of three parts aggression and one part technique, the quaterback had three, filling him with eight parts technique and two parts survival. As this is the way of all quarterbacks, he also drove a Trans-AM sports car and went out with the prettiest cheerleader, a blonde, while the rest of us drove battered old Fords and went out with . . . but that's another story.

The coaches put ten times more effort into him than they did us, because he was ten times more important than us. Coach Jones's explicit instructions to me before every game were: 'Peeete, if you have to die to protect John (the quarterback), don't hesitate to make the sacrifice.' Yes, boss.

But I hated that fancy-pants schmuck. While there were any number of Hogs to replace me, there was only one John Kidd. Coach Jones held the maxim: 'As goes the quarterback, so goes the team.'

I often thought that what I really would like to have done, just one time, was to whisper to the opposing lineman: 'Listen, fathead, on the next play I'm going to take a big dive and leave you a clear run to the quarterback. Make sure you give him a good one for me.' I never did.

But let me leave you with this (it came to me one time after I had just been trashed into the mud by a 300 lb lineman): If ever I could have persuaded my fellow Hogs all over America to rise against their oppressors to seize power, to share alike whatever joys the game had to offer, and caused the revolution to take hold, then eventually I could have turned American football into something like rugby union. Not exactly all power to the Hogs, but at least half the power.

Thank You for Your Warm Welcome

THANK YOU VERY MUCH. I have to admit I'm a little bit nervous . . . never having given a formal after-dinner speech before, let alone to a big city law firm like yours. So nervous, in fact, that while driving here tonight I couldn't help but recall the worst speech of all time, which I'm sure you all remember, but I'll run it by you anyway.

Remember the scene?

It's at the opening of the Los Angeles Olympics and Ronald Reagan has just staggered to the podium with that very, very vague look on his face . . .

Then as the Olympic flag waves in the breeze, the American president starts in . . .

'Mmmmm,' he says, a little uncertainly, 'errr . . . ohhhh.'

'Mr President, Mr President,' a tinny voice can just be heard over the ensuing empty crackles, 'you must read your *cue cards*, Mr President.'

The light of confidence and relief breaks out on Reagan's face anew as he starts in again, gazing into the middle distance.

'Ohhh,' he says, 'Ohhh . . . Ohhh . . .'

'Mr President, you moron,' hisses the urgent voice, 'you're reading the Olympic flag.'

(Pause for, hopefully, peals of laughter.)

But let me just say before continuing . . . I hope you won't think me rude if I say that I can discern right away just that little bit of disappointment coming from you at my presence here tonight. I'm sure a lot of you are disappointed to find that not some eminent jurist is addressing you, but instead just a simple humble footballer. Unless I miss my guess, you'll be taking it as just another sign of the macho culture that prevails in your law firm, that it really is no more than a boys' club, and that my being here addressing you is proof positive of that.

Look, I'm with you . . .

I want to say right away, I feel *exactly* the same way about football. I hate it too. True. And I know you doubt that, because while some people have a face that looks lived in, I have a face that looks lived *on,* and I guess I do appear a bit rough . . . But I'm really sensitive inside all this, I really am.

When I first started to play the rugby game, trying out for the Knox Grammar School U/12 team on their old no. 2 oval, I was profoundly shocked and in *tears* at the end of the first half. Running around, scrabbling all over each other, bleeding, sweating, all for a lousy bit of pumped up leather that was nothing much in particular.

I remember coming off and saying to the coach, 'Please sir, why why can't we ALL have a ball?'

But the brute wouldn't be in it, my proposed revolution came to nought, and I reluctantly had to continue with the traditional mode of the game . . .

So I'm not a proponent of that macho culture, honest I'm not.

And what I really want to say—and this is important—is that a lot of us big boofy males *also* suffer from the work environment macho culture. No kidding. Not so long ago I was just minding my own business, when the phone rang.

'Hello? Mr FitzSimons?'

'Yes,'

'John Singleton would like to speak to you, will you hold

please?' (What could I do? I sat up straight and waited patiently.)

Then Mr Singleton came on the line.

'Hello, Fitzy mate?' (This from a man I'd never met or talked to in my life.)

'Er, yes?'

'Mate . . . ha, ha, ha . . . you sure looked pretty buggered running around on the box the other night . . . ho, ho, ho . . . I wasn't sure if you were going to make it, ho, ho, ho . . .'

'Yes, uh, John, ha (!?!), ha (!?!), ha, ha, I sure was buggered . . .'

On and on it went in this vein. Somehow, after twenty seconds we were speaking with the familiarity of old friends. A minute passed and we were like brothers. After two minutes I had the distinct impression that if my mate Singo had come by the knowledge that I needed a kidney transplant, he wouldn't have hesitated more than a split second to give me one of his, under the auspices of the Really Old Mates Act. Call me a gullible fool if you like, but it was 'male bonding' over the phone *par excellence*, with all the work done by him, and when the time came I was more than primed for the kill.

'So anyway, maaaaate . . . we're doing a promo shot, on a non-commercial basis, for *Cleo* about househusbands, and we needed the ugliest mug we could find . . . so I immediately thought of you . . . ha, ha, ha.'

What it involved was for me to dress up as a caricature of a housewife, with apron and curlers and the whole deal while they took shots of me from every angle bar up my left nostril. For no money. For publication in a national magazine.

Could anything be more excruciatingly embarrassing?

'Sure, John, mate, if I can help you out in any way I'd be very happy to.' (What could I do? I knew full well by this time the guy would have kicked in a kidney for me if I'd needed it, so what was a little photo in return?)

'Great, Fitzy, our people will be in touch to organise times and dates. Thanks. Bye.'

Click.

And who was that masked man anyway?

How could it be that on the strength of a three-minute

phone call, I'd readily agreed to do something so contrary to my real wishes it was breathtaking?

Because of the prevailing macho culture, that's why. See, he *was* John Singleton after all, and he was now an Old Mate . . .

Visions came to me of Singo's secretary providing him with thirty names and numbers at the beginning of each day, together with what was wanted from them, and then him very skilfully firing off Ocker charm torpedoes over the phone, and one by one blowing each and every one of us out of the water.

Was this the quintessentially Australian way of doing business? Is this the way Bondy, Skasey and Holmes á Courty first created their billions? To create in two minutes a strong atmosphere of Old Mateship, and then quickly invoke the Old Mates Act, before signing off with a quick slap on the back?

Whatever it was, it was devastatingly effective and I was almost powerless to stop it. For me, it took a good six hours of rational, analytical and logical progress, step by step in my head, to make headway against the overwhelming feeling that I couldn't let down such a tried and true Old Mate. Finally, I decided I really didn't want to be photographed in such a fashion.

Even then, it took three schooners and a lot of anguish before I worked up the courage to totally betray ol' Singo and make the call to renege on my promise.

I still hate myself for doing it to him and I know I'll never be able to look him in the eye . . . again. But I have every confidence that Singo will go a long, long way, regardless. Even on one kidney.

And I don't know, but I suspect he was more able to do that because he was a knockabout bloke, and I was a knockabout footballer. But I never really wanted to be one of those. HONEST! What I really wanted to be was a lawyer, like you people. Because I always had this wonderful image of lawyers, as opposed to footballers. When I thought lawyer, I thought sleek, well-groomed, affluent, a kind of intelligent, powerful in-control look on their face, much as you all look now. And when I thought footballer, I thought gnarled, scarred, scruffy around the edges, facial features all blurring into one another—much as *I* am now. As a matter of fact I really set out to be one of you, and started studying law as part of an arts degree at Sydney University.

I tried, God knows I tried.

Initially, as a matter of fact, I was able to cope in legal exams quite well—by using a principle I'd learned in algebra at school. If in doubt, if you really just can't work it out, are completely stumped, try X=2. Honest, it always worked for me, right up until about Year Ten when it all started to get a bit difficult . . .

At least in my early days at university, I pursued much the same system with great effect. I'd do my best to work it out, but if I was in any real trouble and had no clue, I'd write down 'as demonstrated by the fundamental principle enunciated by the *Boilermakers'* case' or . . . 'this point was clearly demonstrated by the *Carbolic Smoke-ball Company case.*'

It was a bit like that famous Charlie Brown comic strip, where in a conversation he had with Linus about true and false tests, Charlie Brown told Linus that it was all very easy—teachers always start with a TRUE, followed by a FALSE, and then just to trick you they go back to a FALSE again, then three TRUES in a row . . .

I used to examine past exam papers and much the same pattern would emerge.

The examiners would start with a question to which the answer could be found in the famous *Boilermakers'* case, go to the *Carbolic Smoke-ball Company, case and then three straight Boilermakers'* in a row—*wham wham wham*. And so on.

(They liked it! They liked it!)

Eventually I learned about a few other cases to get me by, but in the end when I did start to get the most basic hang of it, I found the law to be very similar to a sort of spot fire spreading out in the bush every which way from where you stand. As a lawyer you had to charge around wrapping it up, containing it, trying to put the fire out. Making it neat, making it tidy.

And there were always, ALWAYS just endless goddamn *details* to worry about, more little wisps of fire breaking out here and there where you thought you'd put it completely out.

Never knowing, as a lawyer, if one of those little wisps of smoke would turn into flames that would engulf both you and your case. I hated that.

The only thing I did love in the whole thing was the basic principles. Nice, neat, tidy, lovely. Little spot fire, right there, BAM, put it out right under your foot and Bob's your uncle.

'For a valid contract, you need offer, acceptance and considera- tion.'

What could be more simple than that? Easy to under- stand, lovely, bee-yooo-diful.

But who was the mongrel who thought of all the EXCEP- TIONS to these basic principles? And who was the greater mongrel who thought of the exceptions to the exceptions, and the exceptions to the exceptions to the exceptions to the exceptions . . . And it always ended up with you, the nascent lawyer, charging around like a lunatic trying to beat out all these new spreading spot fires with your gum-tree branches till your face turned blue.

In the end, I must admit, I said 'forget it, I'll get my arts degree and become a footballer, that's what I'll do. Farewell to the law, farewell forever, that sort of thing . . .'

(Pause, to hopefully milk a few more laughs out of having a suitably tragic expression on my face.)

Even then, as a footballer, I very nearly missed out on the greatest glory of all, which is to play Test rugby. After years and years of trying, and one false start, I finally got back on board for a major Wallaby tour, on this occasion going to Canada and France. And of course I was entirely delighted to play the first game of that tour, a provincial match in Canada, and to wear the green and gold jersey for the first time in five years.

That night, in a bar, I was waxing lyrical to my friend Tommy Lawton, the most gargantuan hooker international rugby has ever produced, about how *moving* I'd found the whole thing; to stand arm in arm on a foreign field singing the national anthem, about to do battle with the foreign foe . . .

'Wasn't that just so moving for you too, Tommy?' I enthused a little breathlessly.

Tommy, who'd played forty-one Tests to my none, snorted, I mean really *snorted*, then started in. You know what Tommy's like, little slits of eyes, no neck at all . . .

'Mate,' he said, 'I'll tell you what *'moving'* is . Moving will be
if you play a Test match in France and they play the national
anthem and the fifteen of you can only just hear the tune of the
band against the voices of the 70,000 froggies that are
screaming for your blood, but you all belt it out anyway and
you line up to receive the kick-off and you can see this little
sliver of white coming at you end over end like it's in slow
motion and you take it and get belted by four of them, but your
mates close ranks to protect you and you drive them backwards
and you form the first scrum with your blood just trickling
down your nose onto your lip and your eyebrow's swelling up
and you can see the grass about three inches from your eyeballs
and you feel this *massive* heeeeeave coming from behind you
and that . . . THAT is what MOVING is mate. . . .!!!'

*(Some like it, some don't, gotta get 'em all back on board with a bit
of quick self-deprecation.)*

No, I had no idea of what he was talking about either . . . and
still don't. But I *did* get to play the Tests.

The great thing, though, the really great thing, about football
was touring.

There is a saying in the Wallabies, that a rugby tour is a lot
like sex—when it's good it's great, and when it's bad, yeah . . .
well, it's STILL pretty good.

And that's a fair enough saying, for mine. As a matter of fact,
it was a rugby tour that took me to France for the first time,
gave me my first real look at what that country was all
about. I returned there the following year to play and live in a
village down in the south of France by the name of
Donzenac.

Donzenac was a part of France, the French themselves
called *la France profonde, la France authentique*, a place where
there were no super highways, no TGV, McDonald's stores or
Pizza Huts or whatever, a place where the people lived in the
ashes of their ancestors, essentially the same way they had
for centuries past.

*(Good, moving on to some slightly more philosophical ground
here, gotta change the tone just a little. They seem to be coming with
me.)*

Everything there was different to the way I had known it in Australia. A small example, was their approach to medicine. In Donzenac, if you had a wart on the back of your hand, you would not go and see the doctor or whoever, you'd simply cut an onion in two, rub one half of it on the wart, then bury it in the back garden. They believed that by the time the onion had rotted the wart too would have dropped off.

Similarly, if you had a burn, you wouldn't go to pharmacist for some ointment, but would instead go to see the oldest man in the village, Jean-Jacques, and get him to gently blow on it. They believed, I mean really *believed*, that by blowing like that, ol' Jean-Jacques could *enlever le feu*, take away the fire. And be damned if it didn't work. On two occasions I was present when it happened. Little kids crying desperately, and then stopping when Jean-Jacques blew on their burns.

Finally, as an example, they believed that if you were going bald, the only cure was to paste your head with a thin layer of chicken droppings and leave it there for two days . . . *(It's coming, surely it's coming, someone's going to yell it, here it comes . . .)*

'IT SURE DIDN'T WORK ON YOU!'

(Got him.)

Well, you shoulda seen what my hair was like before I did it . . .

Haw. Haw. Haw.

(OK, they're still with me. Gotta follow up with something a bit different again.)

The only real problem there was the referees. There is another saying in the Wallabies—if you'll excuse the vulgarity but I can do no more than tell the truth—that 'the five most useless things in the world are the Pope's balls and three cheers for the ref'.

And never a truer word spoken, I'm here to tell you.

I mean it. I stand before you as one who suffered more than his fair share at the hands of rugby referees over the years, and I think I have legitimate cause for complaint. But the greatest case of refereeing injustice I ever heard of was a former All Black forward by the name of John McIntosh who played in France a couple of years before me. Being an All

Black, the only way he knew how to play the game was to charge into ruck after ruck, maul after maul, get his feet spinning like the back wheel of a motorbike, and start to spit out the bloodied French bodies at the end of his boots.

This was quite legitimate under the rules, but the French referee, being French, just kept penalising him continually until ten minutes before the end of the game the ref had had enough and really blew on his whistle as if his lungs would burst.

'Une fois de plus comme ca, les douches!' he said. One more time I see you rucking like that, it's straight to the showers, you'll be sent off. McIntosh took that on board, but in the end he simply couldn't help himself. With five minutes to go, there was a ruck about ten metres out from the opponent's line and McIntosh hurled himself into it . . . and did the business. Round and round went his feet, and out and out came the French bodies.

The referee blew his whistle, pointed to the dressing-rooms, and with all the venom he could muster belted it out: *'Les douches!'* To the showers, you've been sent off.

McIntosh, disciplined All Black that he was, in that precise instant lost all control, hauled himself up off the turf, and in that cold, calculating Clint Eastwood type voice, turned to the referee and said to him: 'You're a *donkey*. You're a dead-set donkey!'

The referee, entirely unmoved, drew himself up to his full height, and replied: 'It is too late for zee apologies now, my friend.'

(Got 'em, but I don't want to push it. Gotta move away from football and move on to something else.)

And I guess, all up, I'd have to say that football was all right for a while, but what I decided I really wanted to get into was journalism—there were fewer brawls, and the working conditions were a whole lot better.

I'd started writing a few rugby stories for the *Sydney Morning Herald*, but my first really big break was when they gave me a column called 'The Wilds of France' where I reported on the weekly goings on in my lost French village.

I dunno, I guess it played pretty well back home because in the high-placed and frenetic life of Sydney, stories from a sleepy French back-lot were soothing or something. In the end, those columns received such a good reaction I thought I might as well take the opportunity to ride home on their wave and get myself a full-time job on the *Herald*.

I suppose I could have stayed on living in France indefinitely, I loved it so much, but I was finally persuaded that it really was the right thing to do to return, by a line I read in a short story by that greatest of great French writers, Guy de Maupassant, where he said, and I quote: 'It was not four years of experience, so much as one year of experience repeated four times over . . .'

And that was the story of my time in France, *exactly*. It was all wonderful, but repeated wonderful.

Home, James, and don't spare the horses, like my father used to say.

Since then, I hope it won't sound trite if I say that I've enjoyed it all immensely. My pin-up quote of all time about the journalism trade is, 'that the art of journalism is the art of lending to people or events that are intrinsically dull an interest that do not properly belong to them'.

I love that, although I should say I've been fortunate in doing a lot of my writing in sport, where you don't have to work too hard to find interesting stuff. Australia is a good country in which to write about sport, such is the national passion for it.

As an example, I'm sure most of us of certain age here know exactly where we were and what we were doing at the time of the first landing on the moon. A friend of mine was telling me the other day his own story, how he was driving around down Nowra way, desperately trying to pick up a live report on the radio, when suddenly the great horseracing station Radio 2KY came through, clear as a bell. He was just in time . . .

Neil Armstrong himself, speaking: 'That's one small step for man, one giant . . *RAAAACING NOW AT MORUYA* . . .!' That's what came over the radio anyway, as 2KY was off and running into the horserace while Armstrong was left standing.

Good 'ol 2KY—if it's not true, it bloody well ought to be.

(True not strictly indicative of the Australian obsession with sport, so much as horseracing, but they don't seem to have noticed. Still, better not

push this too much, better wrap it up.)

And it's gone pretty well since. There have been other pleasures in journalism, too—palling around with a lot of interesting people and the occasional great person is one of them. Just this last week, as a matter of fact, I've been trying to organise a major profile of Gough Whitlam, and asked him if I could do an in-depth interview with him.

He gracefully declined, but I decided to press on anyway, and said well, if you won't be in that, Mr Whitlam, is there any chance I could organise a lunch with say, you, me and . . . Sir Garfield Barwick?

No, of course, I didn't think it likely that Mr Whitlam would agree to have lunch with the former High Court Chief Justice, the same one who gave Sir John Kerr the informal legal advice that he really did have the constitutional power to sack Whitlam, but it was worth a try . . . .

Anyway, without the barest pause Mr Whitlam replied, in that curiously breathy voice of his 'Well, that would be all right comrade, but you're going to have to get some very very long spoons'. *(Laugh, laugh, laugh, please laugh . . .!)*

Thank you, and good nighhhhhhhht!

Rules of Thump

FOR NO GOOD reason that anyone could ever discern, this bloke broke the schooner glass against the bar and then jabbed the other guy's throat. The blood flowed, and within a minute he was dead.

Which was why we were there. Our mission, should we decide to accept it, was to ensure that nothing of the like ever occurred again. The security of the customers at the league's club had to be ensured at all costs, and the people selected for the job were a collection of five footballers, of which I was one.

Thus began two or three years of weekend bouncing. It was an odd job. As with a fireman at the airport, it quickly became clear that for 99.99 per cent of the time, our task was simply going to be to hang around, look big, and wait for something to happen. All of which I was eminently qualified for. It so happens that 'hanging around' is my strong suit, and at 120 kg and two metres tall, I had the looking-big side of things well covered. It was the 'waiting for something to happen' that was the hard part.

I mean, in three whole years, there was one incident, count 'em . . . *one incident* in which there was a whiff of violence in the air. Some guy, crazy as a loon, had pushed over a table and charged for the door and, of course, half-crazed for action after all those years of waiting for a plane to crashland on the tarmac, all five of us charged through the door after him. It was John who caught up with him first, and popped him one on the chin—in response to which, he fell down.

There was no actual reason I can think of now for John to hit him, but there it was. The guy shortly got up and received a good talking to from all five of us about the inherent naughtiness of pushing tables over in crowded league's clubs, and then he went on his way, rubbing his jaw.

All of which explains in a way, I think, a story I recently read about a young man who was severely beaten by a group of bouncers after he had made the mistake of imitating the band's go-go dancer . . .

'The bouncers dragged me backstage, where other bouncers joined in, giving me a severe beating,' he recounted. 'I fell to the floor. I was then dragged down the backstairs and the back of my head violently struck each step. When I reached the bottom I was barely conscious and the bouncers started kicking me in the head and body until I lost consciousness. I have a very strong constitution, which is why I could stand such a beating. If they had treated anyone more fragile in the same manner, they would have killed him.'

Shocking stuff and no excuse for the way the bouncers behaved. But the explanation is the one I hope I've already sketched. Testosterone and male bonding being what they are, I can well imagine how one over-aggro bouncer popped off the first shot and the others, also hankering after some action, joined in. All bouncers together in the macho fraternal brotherhood; the other bouncers, no doubt, didn't hesitate. One in, all in, right or wrong—*whack*!

Animals of the moment who, I suspect, when they had pause, would have regretted it. But it was precisely because of that sort of stuff and the terrible reputation that bouncers generally suffer that my next brainwave struck . . .

Why not, I asked myself, form my own bouncing company, consisting only of guys who would be guaranteed good talkers with a particular predilection for not belting people? A revolutionary idea and one that I thought had no little merit.

Fifty printed T-shirts, and a lot of strutting around like the new Alan Bond later, Allied Security got its first job— ensuring the security of one thousand or so odds and sods attending a concert by The Trogs at the University of New South Wales Roundhouse.

The funny thing was that when the guy kicked in the plate-glass door, I was only about a metre from him. I was just reaching out to stop this obviously drunken bloke from doing something silly, when he let fly with all the enthusiasm of Maradona scoring the winning goal of the 1986 World Cup final. Wham, wham; tinkle, tinkle, tinkle.

This guy got another good talking to about the inherent naughtiness of kicking in plate-glass windows—on the very night I was launching myself as the new Alan Bond of the bouncing world—but it appeared to make very little impression. So I belted him. No, just kidding—I had one of my fellow bouncers escort him to one of the as yet unbroken doors and that was that.

With him went the entire prestige of my fledgling organisation. Any good bouncer should have an aura shimmering just over his shoulder blades of being in total control of the situation, mixed with just a hint of menace to give the aura a little substance. Both were blown away entirely as I searched for a dustpan and broom to clear away the shards of glass.

Needless to say, the organisers were equally unimpressed with my revelation that, hey, I was only a metre away when he did it. But Allied Security got its first payday, anyway. After paying the others, there was a hundred and fifty dollars left over for me. I bet Bondy didn't make that much on his first signwriting job.

The next job was at Wesley College, Sydney University . . .

How was I meant to know that a group of fifty drunken yobbos would force an entrance through Purser Wing at the precise moment my man was away on a toilet break? What am I, psychic?

No, I am not. Nor did I prove to be much of a businessman. Allied Security went the same way that Bondy's signwriting business did, except that its managing director, *moi*, didn't then go on to make billions. But nor did I then go on to *lose* billions, so I guess Bondy and I turned out even-stevens in the end. I left the bouncing to the real bouncers, the ones that actually bounce people, and that was that.

I don't miss it.

Hitchhiking for Ugly People

HITCHHIKING IS UNDOUBTEDLY the second oldest form of long distance travel. As soon as the first smart caveman got himself organised enough to tame the first dumbo dinosaur, put a vine through its mouth to use as a rein and head it off towards yonder hillock, he undoubtedly came across the second caveman, thumb out, wanting a ride. 'Yonder hillock' were perhaps the words on the little sign held in the second caveman's other hand, and either the dinosaur driver stared the other way at the precise moment of passing by, or he did the right thing and stopped—meaning the two cavemen would have happily headed off towards the hillock together.

Since then hitchhiking has made a good deal of piggyback progress, getting better and faster with each succeeding mode of transport, but the essence remains the same. As a mode of travel at the bottom end of the market, there is no better method than hitchhiking, but there is a rather awkward catch.

If you are on the 'pretty' end of the human spectrum, getting a lift is never any problem but the dangers involved at the hands of assorted crazies make the risk never worth it. If, on the other hand, you are on the rough, tough and 'orrible end of the spectrum, the danger is a lot slighter, but people are infinitely less inclined to pick you up. Unless you do it right.

Even as a fresh-faced youth of eighteen, I was nudging up against the 'orrible end of the spectrum, and initially my only chance of someone stopping was if Mum happened to be passing along the road at the time. Until I learnt how to do it right . . .

The art of 'hitchhiking for uglies' is the art of persuading people travelling at high speed to decide, in the space of a split second, that they should stop and pick you up. Here are a few rules of thumb for hitchhiking . . .

- Let us say you are heading from Sydney to Brisbane. *Don't* hold up a sign saying 'Brisbane'. In fact, don't hold up any sign at all. If your target is actually heading to Brisbane, they may well recoil at the prospect of being with someone for the next ten hours, but wouldn't mind the company of someone for an hour or so. Once you're in the car, you can then charm them into taking you the whole way. If, on the other hand, they are only going to Wyong, they may well surmise that such a short distance isn't of any use to you, when in fact, it is. When hitching, remember—all forward movement is good movement.
- *Don't* hang out a desultory thumb and walk with a hangdog expression along the road. You don't deserve to be picked up that way, because you're obviously a dummy. Use a little amateur psychology here, Sigmund. The only person you care about is the person who can put their foot on the brake, the driver.
- *Do* look the driver straight in the eye, establishing contact. As you lift your arms out into a supplicatory pose, your big, bright, open and honest smile stops momentarily as your lips mouth the words 'Can I have a lift please . . .?' Then quickly back to the smile.

    As you do this, ideally your eyebrows should start to crawl all the way up your forehead. This is the best way known to look beseeching, bright, open and honest all at once.

- *Don't* look like you've just got out of Long Bay Gaol. Even Uglies can be neat, and it's worth making the effort. It may sound bizarre, but the only time my friend Footrot ever wears a tie is when he's hitching. Even if the seat is out of his pants, the tie gives him a Charlie Chaplinesque faded gentility, and he never has any trouble. When the traffic is fair, these methods will get you a lift every time. When the traffic is down to two cars an hour or so on a lost and lonely highway, you need ever more refined methods.

Once, out on a patch of the Nullarbor, I set down just near another hitchhiker. Skeletons in the dust told us both that this was Hitchhiking Hell, but the etiquette of the road still counted. I had to retire a good kilometre or so beyond him so he would get first shot.

Luckily he was a dummy.

Putting his pack down against a post, he sat against it and lifted a languid stick every time a car passed. Despite the heat, the flies, his hunger and thirst, he didn't really look as if he wanted to get out of there. His folly was my saviour. By the time people had passed him, leaving him in the desert, they would invariably be feeling guilty. I, too, would be sitting down, but when the cars were about five hundred metres off, I would suddenly jump up—which attracted their attention—and look really excited as if *finally* they had come to save me ('der plane, boss, der plane!').

All right, it still took me half a day to get out of there, but even the people who didn't stop at least slowed down and took a good, long hard look at me. The point is to view the whole operation not as 'hitchhiker and passing cars' but as 'hitchhiker and passing *people*', and then take it from there.

Incidentally, one more special pleasure of the road to look out for, particularly in parts where it is difficult to get a lift, is hitchers' poetry, often seen carved onto the back of road signs with a rock or somesuch. A personal favourite, on the back of a sign on a dead stretch of road about a hundred kilometres out of Katherine in the Northern Territory (and I think the same was written by a thumbnail dipped in tar), goes like this:

We met,
We slept,
She left,
I wept.

It's not Dylan, but it's not bad.

Meeting the President

THAT WAS FUNNY, he certainly didn't *look* like Jimmy Carter. Yet that was how he insisted we address him, so we did. Standing in the shade of the mighty King Cheops Pyramid, which lies on the western edge of Cairo, the man who had called himself after an American President was an old and wizened man. He wore the long flowing robes that most Egyptians seem to favour and a perpetually amused look that is rather rarer in the people of that nation. Jimmy had by a lead a camel of absolutely breathtaking ugliness—even by a camel's usual standards.

It was only half an hour earlier that the sun had risen, and if we could just get rid of Jimmy, my friend Richard and I were anxious to begin our ascent of the pyramid before it became too cripplingly hot. And sure, there were 'Forbidden to Climb', 'Verboten!', 'Il est interdit de grimper' signs everywhere, but these didn't trouble us unduly. It was too early in the day for there to be any security of note, and both of us were enthusiastic to get to the summit come what may.

42

Richard had wanted to climb the Pyramid ever since he was a little kid in New York. For myself, having grown up with a photo around the farmhouse of my dad with his slouch-hat atop Cheops during an R & R break from El Alamein in the Second World War, it also seemed kinda nice that I get to the top some forty years later.

For his part Jimmy Carter was also keen that we climb the pyramid, it's just that he wanted each of us to pay him twenty American dollars cash to keep a lookout for any cops or officials that might be passing by.

Sure, Jimmy, pull the other one. Now wouldn't you much rather take your camel for a quick canter around yonder sandhills so a couple of tourists can get about their business? But Jimmy wouldn't hear of it. With a charming smile, and the Sphinx as sombre back-up looking grimly over his shoulder, Jimmy kept insisting that we absolutely *had* to have someone keeping lookout and though he'd like to, he simply couldn't find his way clear to come down in his price.

'Itth twentth dollarth,' the old man said. 'I'llth thbe yourth lookoutth.'

He had a funny way of speaking, Jimmy did, sort of chewing on every word before letting it out of his mouth and if you didn't know better you'd swear he'd learnt this manner of speaking from his camel. I say that, because both Rich and I couldn't help noticing that the camel's jaws seemed somehow psychically connected to the old man's, as they both chewed away in perfect time, whether speaking or not. It was weird.

But anyway . . . sure, Jimmy, sure.

The sun began to climb, giving us a double whammy as it bounced up off the sand, and the negotiations became more protracted. Jimmy simply wouldn't budge from his demand of twenty dollars, wouldn't go away, and finally it occurred to both Rich and me almost simultaneously: 'What the hell do we owe this guy anyway?' After all, just what was he going to do to stop us? So . . .

'Get stuffed, Jimmy,' we said, all but in unison, as we set off up the first huge steps of the pyramid. We got to maybe only the third step before Jimmy took his weapon out. Its sleek silver metal glinted in the sun. With a chewy kind of smile, Jimmy raised it . . . and blew.

A long piercing wail bounced around between the pyramids. As whistles went it was a particularly loud and piercing one.

And Jimmy had us cold, no doubt about it. No guards had come running yet, but it took perhaps three or more times gumption than either Rich or I had to continue to climb with Jimmy leaning on the whistle. There was only one thing to do.

So anyway, Mr President, how would you like that twenty bucks, in ones, fives, or tens?

'Fiveth pleathe,' said Jimmy, the camel momentarily slowing his chews to allow him to get the words properly out, before they both resumed at their normal rate.

With our wallets lightened, we set off back up the pyramid as Jimmy and his camel wandered away, another excellent morning's work completed.

So we climbed. Each step seemed about a metre high, though occasionally the height varied to about half that. Most of the time it meant scrambling upwards on hands and knees rather than actually stepping out, and the sort of solid sandstone of which it was made seemed particularly well designed to bark one's shins, so we did just that.

Involved in such strenuous exertion on such a monument, at least minor philosophical thoughts occur to you and we didn't miss our mark.

All up, there seemed only two basic ways of looking at the pyramids. The standard form is 'wonder'—wonder at man's early achievement, being able to build such a stupendous structure at such an early time in history, without the aid of slide-rules, measuring tapes or even a mid-sized front-end loader.

The other perspective is rather less popular, but no less pertinent—aghast. Aghast at what the pyramids truly represent in terms of human suffering.

As glorified gravestones go, these pyramids were pretty glorious, sure, but the work! The sweat, the strain and monumentally agonising effort they represent is truly appalling. After twenty minutes, and still not in sight of the top, Rich and

I stopped for a breather—absolutely dripping with the mere effort of hauling the weight of our bodies to this point.

What, we wondered, must have been involved in getting two tonnes of rock up to the same level? And who were the poor bunnies born to this world only to find that their destined role was to haul chunks of stone directly opposite gravity's pull, all with the aim of giving another bloke an impressive grave?

It wasn't quite that when we got to the top, the view was *entirely* ruined for us, but it had certainly palled somewhat.

Bummer.

A Road Death

IT'S VERY ODD, how disengaged one can be even in the presence of death. This guy had just been crossing the road outside our hotel room in Aswan, in Egypt's south, when a truck had come along and killed him, *Boom!*, just like that.

We actually heard the scream of brakes and then a dull kind of thud, and by the time we came out on our balcony to see what was happening, the guy was dead, lying with his head half under one wheel and the blood having already stopped flowing. The driver of the truck was out of his cab, and wailing loudly over the prone figure on the road, and though the first people on the scene prevailed upon him to get back in the truck and at least reverse off the guys' head, it changed the end result not a jot.

As foreigners in a strange land, both Richard and I felt neither the instinct nor the inclination to become involved at such a moment, and so we just stayed on the balcony and dispassionately observed what happened next. Either Aswan didn't have ambulances, or there weren't enough to collect people that were already dead. In about twenty minutes time a sort of pick-up truck with two roughly uniformed types came along, picked the body up, unceremoniously threw it in the back and drove away. The one cop who'd come and asked a few questions saw the body safely on board and then he, too, drove off on his mo-ped.

Then we saw them, approaching like Angels of Death.

Boats coming from across the river. Lots of them. Loaded to the gunnels with ethereal figures in black, the oars on either side being pushed by unseen hands.

These boats, it turned out, were full of Muslim women from the fellow's village, which was directly on the other side of the Nile from us. The first one ashore contained the woman who was undoubtedly the dead man's mother—she ran from the shore to where the blood still lay fresh on the road.

We thought she was going to throw herself on the still wet blood, but she didn't. Instead, she quite calmly gathered some rocks from the side of the road and placed them in a rough outline of the stain, obliging all traffic to drive around the spot where her son had died. Then she began wailing, jigging up and down at the same time. It was an odd rhythmic sort of wail—'Ai, ai, ai, ai, aieeeeeeee!, ai, ai, ai, ai, aieeeeeeee!' And all the while she continued jigging up and down in her long black robes, only her eyes visible over the top of her veil.

By this time, the first of the other boatloads had arrived, and packs of black moved up from the shore to her sound. The newcomers embraced the grieving mother in turn, and then the whole lot of them took up the eerie wail, all jigging up and down in unison. 'Ai, ai, ai, ai, aieeeeee!'

With each arriving boatload, the mother would briefly break from the dense pack to embrace and wail with the newcomers and then the whole lot of them would recommence with renewed vigour.

And still the boats kept coming. All in black, all of them women. It was an entirely inappropriate thought at the time, but they looked like nothing so much as penguins coming up from the shore, waddling in the way their heavy robes obliged them to, and then commencing their wailing and jigging when first they made contact with the mother. In the end there must have been two hundred of them, still going strong about an hour later, when the last boat had arrived.

Presently, they moved off down the street, presumably to go and find the actual body of the woman's dead son. It was about half a kilometre before they turned the corner, and even at that distance we could still hear them clearly.

The following morning, the blood stain was still there. And so were the rocks. And so was the mother. Not jigging now. Not wailing. Just squatting by the side of the road and staring at the spot. She had her hands up to her mouth and they would just occasionally, languidly, brush away a fly before returning to her lips.

I was going to walk with Richard to the station before going myself to catch the boat across the Aswan Dam to the Sudan, and the direct route would have taken us right by the grieving woman.

We took the long way.

The Sudan Train

IT WAS PROBABLY the putrid smell from my boot, being used as a pillow beneath my head, that woke me. Or simply swollen-tongued thirst. Or that, in the night, the train had once again stopped moving. Whatever, I was now wide awake and very uncomfortable.

Attempting to roll over just a little brought such aggressive grunts from the six Sudanese men I was attached to that, in the end, I just lay there sweating quietly and took stock of my position. I was on a train straight out of hell, stopped in the northern reaches of the Sudan, nominally two days' travel to the north of Khartoum.

The only water available on my carriage was a greenish brew in an almost empty barrel. I hadn't eaten for a day or slept more than one hour of the last twenty-four. Not that that was surprising. Sleeping in the valley between two railway seats was never going to be easy when a fair portion of one's 'mattress' was the six pairs of bare black feet of the men sitting on the seats above, trying to sleep. But with sixty of us packed in this carriage designed for thirty, there was nothing for it.

It was the summer of '85. A month earlier I'd finished a season of playing rugby in Italy and was now travelling from Cairo to Cape Town overland. *From* Cairo because that was the easiest access point to Africa from Europe; *to* Cape Town because that was the country where this girl called Jenny lived; and overland because that seemed the cheapest and most adventurous way.

With the possible exception of the Ugandan jungles, the Sudanese desert always looked to be the most difficult section of the trip. Fine. But *this* difficult?

The map showed a train line starting from a little town in the north of the Sudan and going all the way south to Khartoum. I reasoned that if I got on this train, and this train proceeded along this line, then I simply must emerge at Khartoum, some time soonish. And what an example of addled Western reasoning that turned out to be.

For this was a *Sudanese* train. It did far more stopping than proceeding. It stopped on the edge of every town so that an emissary could go forward on foot to ask whichever warlord was in charge that week for permission to let the train pass. It had to stop five times a day so that all the Muslims on the train (everybody except me) could kneel, face Mecca and pray for fifteen minutes. It had to stop every time it broke down, which was often, and it had to stop many times for no apparent reason whatsoever.

And right now it was stopped. Again.

There was a movement along the passageway, and a voice hissed.

'Mr Peter, we walking up to next town for more water. Come?'

It was my one 'friend' on the train, Mahmad. He liked me because he loved nothing better than beating white men at chess, and I was the only member of that species in a hundred kilometres. I liked him because I just did, that's all, and because I figured it a good policy to have at least one local ally, given my circumstances.

Mahmad informed me that the water barrel was empty

and seeing as the train wouldn't be fixed for at least another twelve hours, he and three of his mates had decided to do what they must to get water. My mouth was so dry it felt as if someone had put the Dead Sea Scrolls in there overnight for safekeeping, so I was keen. We walked quietly along the tracks, trying to pick out places for our feet where we would not stumble.

Three hours later, the dim lights up ahead meant that we had reached the next town. We could see the expected men with guns on the platform, but having come this far we had no choice. Thirst has its own imperatives. And through the many baleful glares and gun muzzles, we spied the water tap.

For reasons I am yet to understand, even though these guys were nasty, armed and obviously assigned to keep the station secure, their only hostile act was to stare nastily at us as we doused ourselves with the water and filled our bellies and canteens to bursting. They didn't even ask for my papers, even though one of the railway workers told Mahmad I was the first white man through there in the past two months. (And maybe he was right, because one little black child burst into tears at the very sight of me.) But enough already—we had finally had our fill.

As we walked back along the tracks, we passed three other groups coming for water and Mahmad gave them the good news that in all likelihood they wouldn't be shot for their trouble. The whole thing stands out as the one happy episode on a truly abysmal trip: not getting shot for getting water.

Three days later, a dark smudge appeared on the horizon: Khartoum. Of course, we had to stop one more time before getting there because some mad mongrel dog of a camel driver simply jumped off the moving train; we had to go back and get his broken-legged body back on the beast, but we were all past caring. We could smell Khartoum up ahead in the wind and that was all that mattered.

Khartoum

PEOPLE WHO'VE BEEN to Khartoum often say that if God were to give the world an enema then the Sudanese capital city is surely where He would insert the tube. I agree.

Appropriate form when writing about any city is of course to find at least a few redeeming features, somehow, somewhere, so as to give one's account some balance, but when it comes to Khartoum I say the hell with it.

I say Sudan's capital city resembled nothing so much as that part on the very edge of all garbage dumps which is all stinky and blowy—without actually being a part of the garbage dump proper—and the only curiosity in Khartoum's case was that this stinky blowy part went clear from the edges right to the very heart. The place where England's General Gordon came to a rather grizzily end last century is also the place where most visitors have spent almost equally horrible times since.

For myself this was all exacerbated by becoming embroiled in a rather bitter dispute while staying at a fly-blown hostel near the city centre.

On one side was this Australian guy who was the expedition leader of a travel tour on the back of a truck through the back-blocks of Africa. He had chosen that time and that place to abandon his dozen paying customers to fly back to London because as far as he was concerned they could all 'garngetf----!', because he had bloody well had a gutful of them and their constant whingeing.

On the other side were the travellers, who hated his guts and told me that in the three weeks they'd been with him he had yet to shower or even wash, that he made stews at night that would kill a brown dog, and that he somehow, amazingly, managed to drive, pick his pimples, play with his testicles and pick his nose all at the same time and he was far and away the most disgusting human they'd ever met.

I dunno, Bob was a pretty rank sort of person, I suppose.

But on the other hand he *was* an Australian, and his customers were mostly Englanders, so it seemed pretty natural that I try to more or less take Bob's side in the dreadful impasse. It was probably a mistake, seeing as when Bob did fly out, without warning, he also managed to take some of the tour kitty with him and they hated him even more and me by reflection and . . .

And TAXI!

But there were none to be found. Nor was it really possible to hitchhike in those extreme parts.

Fortunately, I heard that by taking a short flight over the worst of the civil war in the south of Sudan, I could land in Juba not too far from the Uganda border, and pay some truck-driving blokes to take me through the Ugandan jungles into Kenya and all the way to Nairobi.

Too easy. Where do I sign?

I found them in a truck-stop on Juba's edge. Two trucks going in a convoy on a four-day trip through Uganda, leaving the following morning at dawn, and for the princely sum of twenty American dollars I would be welcome to go in the first truck.

At first light we were off. The driver's name was Jaat, an

easygoing Somali, and his companion's name was Lasu—
though the latter was so sick with a terrible case of malaria, that
his main communication was through groaning. A short
groan meant he was as happy as could be expected, a long
groan—extremely unhappy. Lasu lay the whole time on the
bunk behind the driver's seat as we travelled south, and
probably vastly worsened his condition because, like his
companions, he refused to take any sustenance at all
between sun-up and sun-down as we were in the holy
Muslim month of Ramadan.

Of course for me, it was in vain to say 'Muslim . . . shmuslim,
where's my food?', because I was entirely obliged to live at their
rhythm, learning as I went.

Like that first night. When we finally sat around the fire and
prepared to eat from the communal food bowl that Jaat had
prepared for us, I learnt a very important lesson. When
dipping your hand into food with a bunch of Somalis in the
Ugandan jungle, NEVER use your left hand. That, I was told in
no uncertain terms, was the hand with which one wipes
one's bottom, and only the feeeelthy son of a leprous camel
would put his toilet hand into a food bowl.

Right. Excuse me. I don't know what I could have been
thinking of.

Apart from that though, they were very friendly, even
Lasu managing to groan once or twice in a warm enough
sort of fashion that evening. But because Lasu was so sick,
Jaat told me that he'd have to remain on the bed in the
truck, while I would have to take Lasu's usual position on
the ground.

And that would be . . . exactly where, Jaat?

'By the diesel tank.'

Right. Both trucks had a diesel tank on each side and the
system was for each guy to sleep beside one so that any
thieves in the night couldn't steal diesel without waking you up.

And so it went. With the two trucks moving further into
Uganda, we settled into a fairly unchanging pattern of
progression.

Each day began at first light, with a gentle nudge on the
shoulder. As I surfaced from the land of nod, Jaat would grin

and pass me an already lit cigarette. It was the Somali version of what outback Australians call 'a dingo's breakfast'—a bit of a scratch, a bit of a stretch, a bit of a look around.

Then we'd set off, grinding along the ruts through the hills of Northern Uganda, stopping every twenty miles or so at a roadblock set up by groups of armed men.

These were a kind of Ugandan toll-gate. At that time Uganda had just been through one of the many military coups that had followed the fall of Idi Amin, and the country-side was full of roaming armed men who'd been part of losing factions (members of the winning faction were in Kampala) and who were trying to live off the land. When they required some cash or food, which was always, they set up a fairly simple roadblock of a couple of logs across the road, with them holding machine guns just behind. Then they'd lighten the traveller's load a little.

Oddly enough, my Somali mates were entirely uncon-cerned by this—for them it was just a normal part of travelling through Uganda, and not to worry, it was only rare that someone actually got shot. Jaat would usually give them a few minor notes of the Ugandan currency, Lasu would groan heavily enough to get a well-deserved sympathy vote, and that left . . . only me.

For obvious reasons I couldn't possibly tell them that I had 1000 dollars in American notes secreted in the lining of my boot, so always had to plead that I only had travellers cheques. They would then fossick around in my backpack for something that interested them and though they could quite easily have taken the whole thing, that wasn't the system. The system was like a real toll-gate, just take something of value and let the people pass on. Oddly enough, despite the fact that they were heavily armed and taking my stuff as of right and not as a favour, they seemed entirely unaggressive about it— there was simply no point in being aggressive because their machine guns said all that needed to be said on the subject and any display of emotion added on top of that would be entirely superfluous.

So it was that each time we'd stop I would be lightened of some deodorant, some socks, a belt, a little loose change, whatever it was that they particularly fancied. A couple of times they seemed rather keen to relieve me of my camera and it took some dissuasion on my part to keep it, but that was all. Merely by my taking photos of them—'now everybody say "cheese" or "Idi Amin's a loser", or something'—with their barrels pointing straight down the lens as they grimaced appropriately, and promising to return in a couple of weeks to show them the photos, they let me go with the camera intact.

So we continued to wend our way south-east, through the thick jungles and occasional villages.

It was on the third night out that we camped just outside a mid-sized town and the boys seemed in the mood for a bit of a party. Never mind that during the day they were absolutely strict about observing the strictures of Ramadan—insofar as not imbibing food or water—come night-time they drank alcohol, smoked marija-hoochy, and chewed on these red betel nuts with an enthusiasm only to be equalled by the enthusiasm with which they didn't sleep.

And this night, I gathered, they wanted to add 'finding a woman' to the list.

'See if you can't bring a lady back for me,' I joked as they left, before settling down for the night beside my diesel tank, which I'd grown rather fond of.

It must have been about one o'clock when I awoke, out of the strangest dream. I was back with my lover and we'd been lying on the bed in the evening light, feeling mellow, and I'd been . . . and then she'd . . . and I'd . . . and . . .

'WHO THE HELL ARE YOU!?!?!?' I hadn't been quite dreaming everything after all. In the moonlight, I could see her, an African girl of perhaps 17 years of age smiling down at me. Most importantly, I could *feel* her—for her highly original method of waking me involved her putting her hand down my sleeping bag and manipulating the more sensitive areas of my nether-nether regions.

Jaat, she said, had told her where she could find me by the tank and as she'd never met a white man she thought she'd take the opportunity. The others wouldn't be back for at least an hour, she said.

It was a worry alright.

The following morning, Jaat woke me just the same, with a lit cigarette and mentioned in passing that we should be reaching the Kenyan border by about midday.

Which in the end, was where I left them. When we got about two kilometres from the border, we hit the tail end of a whole queue of trucks, some of which had been waiting there for two days. For a reason that I couldn't fathom, every truck coming out of Uganda was being minutely searched by the Kenyan authorities and for me the solution was obvious—get my backpack, walk to the front of the queue and get a lift on a truck that had already been passed through. So . . .

See ya, Jaat.

'See you Mr Peter.'

See ya, Lasu.

'Nnnnghhh.'

Lasu was still crook. I myself was feeling better with every step closer to Kenya.

BigJohn

YOU MEET ALL types while hitchhiking, of course, but this was the first time I'd ever met a guy whose proud boast was that he'd 'personally killed 370 people'. And he meant it.

True. I met 'Big John', as he insisted I call him, about a hundred miles inside the Zimbabwe border and travelled with him for a good part of the way to Harare, the capital. He was a big-shouldered sort of bloke, as I remember, with tousled hair, red skin, and the slightly squinty 'n' vacant eyes of one who has spent a lot of time staring outwards on the far plains—without having come to too many conclusions. Or maybe that was just the way I read him, for it turned out John had come to many, many conclusions in his time . . . The first and foremost of these being that the kaffirs were a filthy kind of people who couldn't be trusted to walk in a straight line, let alone run the country, as they were trying to do now, and in his opinion, they'd all be better off dead.

Such a passionate certitude was a promising start to what

would be an interesting trip, because there was no doubt John had a few things on his mind that he was only too eager to unload. There is often an immediate intimacy between hitchhiker and host which means extraordinarily personal conversations ensue. It is an anonymous, glancing acquaintance in a closed environment perfect for conversation, and as the veldt slipped backwards in the late afternoon sun, Big John began to tell me his story.

Like everybody else, when he'd heard Prime Minister Ian Smith say that white rule would continue in Rhodesia for another thousand years, he'd believed him. Of course, he'd had no reason to doubt that the whites, as the master race, would continue to be strong enough to dominate the situation; that they would beat back the rising insurgency of disaffected blacks who thought they could run the country better and more equitably than the whites.

But the war against the rebel blacks had worsened. The kaffirs had begun to attack outlying farms and outposts, then farms closer in, then even the fringes of isolated towns, with the odd attack downtown; soon the call went out for all good strong men and true (which is to say all white men) to go out into the wilderness and beat the heathen back.

To do this, some had gone into the regular Rhodesian Army; some had formed their own kind of militia; and some, like John, had joined this outfit called the Selous Scouts—a kind of specialist force within the army whose job it was to infiltrate enemy territory and create havoc any way they could.

The big thing with the insurgent blacks at that time was to use the neighbouring wilds of Mozambique as a staging post and safe haven from the Rhodesian Army. The blacks, who John called 'terries', short for 'terrorists', would base themselves in Mozambique, slip across the border, make their hit on whatever was their chosen white target, and then get back to Mozambique, where in accordance with international law, the Rhodesian Army couldn't follow.

Which was where John came in. It didn't take him long to find his niche in the Selous Scouts . . .

With his high-powered telescopic rifle and plenty of ammunition, John would paint his body black so as to appear native, at least from a distance, take enough basic food provisions for a week, and then get himself dropped by helicopter up into the far reaches of the Rhodesian wilderness, near a route along which the terries would travel.

He'd then select some suitable high ground with at least one escape route, and wait . . .

And wait some more. And eventually, maybe after as long as two or three days, he would see them coming along the track at perhaps a distance of five hundred metres or so, and he'd line them up . . .

'Usually,' John said, and I can still remember exactly the way he said it, 'I could kill the first two straight out; two bullets out before they knew what was happening, and then I could often at least injure one of the others before they had time to scatter too far and . . .'

Always it was the same thing. Death coming suddenly from the hills, from a direction unknown—one or two dead, and at least one other badly injured. With no idea of how many assailants were out there, the group of terries would be incapable of any sort of action at all for at least half an hour.

Even then . . . if they did try to follow him, and headed towards the hill where they thought he was secreted, it was never with any stomach for the fight. Whoever the sniper or snipers was or were, the terries knew that he had a high-powered gun which he knew how to use, and was only too willing to do so. The end result was that in all his years in the hills John had never come close to being cornered.

Instead, he would usually just shift his position by a kilometre or two under cover of darkness, either on the same track or to a different one, and once again take up position. The crucial thing he always looked for in these positions was height and density of surrounding bush, with hopefully at least one path that approximated an escape route in case he ever did get into trouble. He'd launch another attack or two over the next week and then he would meet the helicopter again at a pre-arranged spot and be airlifted back to safety.

And he was very very good at the whole caper. A bit of a legend in the whole Selous Scouts set-up, he told me, even if he did say so himself . . . So good in fact, that that way of fighting the war became Big John's primary concern and he devoted himself to it over a seven-year period.

Again, I can still remember exactly the way he told me the following:

'I averaged a bit over fifty kills a year, but in my best year I got seventy-five of the bastards.'

Elsewhere, the war raged on. Another primary concern of the Selous Scouts was to capture the terries in order to interrogate them about where exactly their bases were in Mozambique. I can't remember if it was the Selous Scouts themselves or some other outfit that did the interrogations, but one method of interrogation John described to me still sticks in my head all these years later. It involved getting two captured terrorists who wouldn't talk and taking them up in a helicopter.

'You'd ask one of them where the bases were and when he refused to answer you pushed him out the open door of the helicopter. The other one would always talk straight away.'

Hard men, fighting a hard war. When, in the end, it all came to nought, Rhodesia going under and Zimbabwe rising in its place, former fighters like John had to go back to their farms—at least those parts of their farms that hadn't been nationalised and taken over by the new government.

The only thing I couldn't figure was given that he'd done so much damage and killed so many people, why hadn't he fled to South Africa like so many others? And given that he'd stayed, why hadn't the new government effected some dreadful act of retribution? Why hadn't it evened the score a bit for all the killings he'd done? Basically, why hadn't be been dragged from his bed at midnight and killed outright?

He didn't go to South Africa, he said, because it wasn't his country, Rhodesia was, and as for why he hadn't been killed in revenge himself, he wasn't quite sure, but he always slept with a gun near at hand, don't you worry about that. One day, he thought, they'd come for him, and he just hoped to be able to take one or two with him.

I would confess to being just a tad sceptical about the whole story and wouldn't necessarily have believed him quite down to the wire, but as I jumped out of the car he was most insistent: 'When you get to South Africa, find the book *Selous Scouts* by

Lt Col Ron Reid Daly Norman—look me up in the fifth chapter.

Sure enough, when I got to Johannesburg, I did just that, and there he was, with a photo and all.

Like I say, you meet some weird types while hitchhiking . . .

An Odd Episode

SOUND TRAVELS WELL in the African twilight.

I heard the vehicle coming for a full ten minutes before it actually appeared. By the side of a lost and lonely track in the southern reaches of Zimbabwe, I had just begun to eye a large concrete pipe in a culvert as my probable shelter for the night . . . when the rough waves of *rrrRRRrrrRRRRRrrr* through the hum of mosquitoes gave me renewed hope of getting a lift the hell out of there. The dull glow of headlights over the rise showed up next, and presently it appeared—a battered old Landrover nudging its way over the ruts.

Despite my upturned palms and imploring-yet-honest expression of the truly gifted hitchhiker, the vehicle passed me by, slowing only marginally so the three men in the front seat could get a brief look at me. Five hundred metres down the track, though, the Landrover slowed, turned, and came back. 'Where goin'?' the driver asked.

Black faces in semi-darkness mask a person's demeanour well, but this man at least didn't seem hostile. Now that I could see them close-up and stationary, it was apparent the jeep was a kind of police paddy wagon, with the insignia on the men's shoulders identifying them as members of the Zimbabwean police force. Perfect. And surely safe.

'I'm going to the Zambezi River crossing,' I said. 'Can you give me a lift?'

A toss of his head towards the back of the wagon told me that I was to climb in over the tailgate, and after retrieving my backpack, I did so.

In the back of the wagon were four men in the ragged khaki uniforms of the national police and they all nodded at me gruffly as I took my seat on the spare tyre. None of them spoke to me, but I imagined they were wondering, 'What the hell is a lone white man doing in these parts?'

Good question. I was beginning to wonder that myself. Though I wasn't at all afraid at this stage, there was something disquieting which I couldn't quite get a full grip on—like a sense of *déjà vu* that refuses to properly crystallise.

A couple of kilometres down the track, for no reason I could discern, the jeep suddenly stopped. There was a brief conversation from the front, the clunk of metal against metal, and the driver appeared, carrying four rifles.

In the sort of slow-motion time one moves through when profoundly shocked, I managed to ask myself perhaps twenty times, 'What could he *possibly* be carrying four rifles for?'—in the time it took for the driver to hand them out to the men in the back.

Still not a word was spoken to me, and the jeep moved on. It was then that I suddenly remembered, with horror, what had been troubling me. Only two days before, about two hundred kilometres north of Harare, I had been picked up by a member of the Matabele people [Zimbabwe is made up of two oft-warring tribes, the Matabele and Shona] who was still shaking with rage at an atrocity he had just heard had been committed.

I, too, had heard the news of the six German tourists who had just recently been pulled out of their mini-bus and shot dead in a ditch, but it wasn't their deaths directly which out-raged this fellow, so much as his information that they had been murdered by Shona policemen travelling through Matabeleland, apparently in an attempt to severely embarrass the Matabele people.

Oddly enough, I wasn't panicked by this story at the time—in Africa you pays your money and takes your chances. But I *was* doing at least my fair share of panicking now. And then some . . .

Again and again, the thought kept forming: 'I . . . am . . . quite probably . . . going to *die.*'

One time, in India, when I had been foolish enough to smoke something that was not quite straight tobacco, my mind had of its own accord started flip-flopping paranoically between outright panic and a slender grip on calm—*my mind is stuffed*!/I'm OK, keep calm/*my mind is shot to pieces*!!/it'll return to normal soon, just *don't panic*!!!/*I'm stuffed*!!! And so on.

This was a little like that, except in this instance there were no stray chemicals involved; my mind was fighting a battle between straight pant-wetting fear and a semblance of basic calm. On the one hand, no-one had yet made an openly hostile move and there was still no concrete evidence that I was in any sort of real trouble. On the other, I was an unarmed white man alone, on a road that obviously led to South Africa, in the company of armed black men of suspicious intent.

With every kilometre that I didn't get shot dead and left to rot in a ditch, calm was beginning to gain the ascendancy . . . then the truck pulled off the main track and went about five hundred metres up another smaller track, to a small clearing, where it again stopped. A conversation then ensued between the men in the front and the men in the back, and their raised voices indicated rather strong disagreement.

It seems absurd in hindsight, but at such an anxious moment my mind turned not to my family, or lover who awaited me in Johannesburg—but instead to Maxwell Smart, 'Agent 86' of the television series 'Get Smart'. In one of those episodes, I remembered, Max had flicked a burning cigarette into the eyes of one of the dastardly KAOS agents to buy two or three seconds to make good his escape.

It wasn't much, but it was all I had, and even as they

talked, I began furiously chain-smoking, formulating a plan whereby the first bloke to point a gun at me with intent would get a burning Marlboro jammed right in his eye, whereupon I would kick out viciously at another, vault over the backboard and hurtle off into the night. Or maybe I shouldn't even wait, maybe right now I should vault over the truck-gate, sprint like a loon, and take my chances in the African night.

I had just resolved that this was probably the best option of all, when the engine started again and the truck moved back to the main track. There seemed to be three possibilities: they'd changed their minds and weren't going to kill me after all; this particular killing field wasn't to their liking and we were going to another; my whole sense of danger was a product of my fevered imagination.

Amid it all, as we bumped down the track, I was totally mesmerised by the end of the rifle barrel belonging to the man sitting opposite me, which I could just see in my cigarette's glow.

The truck stopped again. The time had come. Now, surely now, they would make a move if they were going to and, by *God*, I was going to jab hard with my cigarette and . . .

And the driver was there at the back of the truck.

'OK, mister, we stop here at police station for tonight. Best you sleep in cell here tonight to be safe.'

We were in fact at a police station outpost in the sticks, and after one of the men who only minutes before I'd thought was likely to kill me had made a rather goodish cup of tea, I passed a reasonably comfortable night in one of the cells. In the morning I moved on, after handshakes all round. One of the cops even flagged me down the next passing truck.

So what the hell had all the rifles and arguments and excursions into clearings been about the previous night?

I still wonder.

Jerry

ON THE NOSE? I guess so. I'd been travelling hard through Africa for the past two months without being able to do anything so luxurious as wash, and my last lift into Johannesburg had brought me all the way from the Zambezi River on the back of a utility truck laden with bales of hay and three dogs. So maybe I did smell a bit.

But from the moment when Mr and Mrs Botha arrived to pick me up in the rough part of Jo'burg in their shiny new Mercedes we just didn't hit it off. They were perfectly polite 'n' all, and even gave me a sniffy handshake—I was, after all, ostensibly the fellow their daughter was in love with—but even after I'd scrubbed myself down and put on one of Mr Botha's shirts, there was still no *warmth*. There was little more than a sparse observance of the correct form for receiving someone who'd travelled ten thousand miles to stay with them.

And my lover in all this?

Jenny resisted being influenced by her parents' feelings for all of five minutes by my count. Only a week later, with the whole relationship in ashes, I knew it was time to get going again. (Incidentally, what was that wonderfully over-the-top line I remembered from that play? *'I don't want to be breaking your heart, gal, but I gotta be travelling on.'* Well, I got the last part right, anyway.)

You'd think it would be pretty easy, wouldn't you, to get from Johannesburg's southern suburbs to stand beside the main highway to Cape Town? Particularly when you knew that a correct destination bus passed by the Bothas' front door every half an hour?

But no. I'd packed my bag, left the Bothas as polite a note as I could manage under the circumstances, and was standing by the bus-stop, at five-thirty am.

The first bus that came along was laden with blacks on their way to work in the whites-only area and as I tried to board, the bus driver, looking most surprised, told me that this was a 'Blacks Only' bus.

'That's all right,' I replied with an airy wave of the hand, 'I don't mind a bit riding with you. You see I'm not a South African and . . .'

And it didn't matter. He still didn't want my business, and he was sure his passengers felt the same.

I looked down the bus and saw that he was right—very hostile faces, all riled at my very presumption in trying to get on their bus.

(*Exit one bus. Leaving hitchhiker standing in a cloud of dust and exhaust fumes, ponderously scratching his head.*)

Well, bugger it. I *was* an Australian, after all, and when all else failed I could always use Shanks's Pony, *walking* the necessary ten kilometres. Which I did.

About two nights later, with the moon high in the sky, I was more or less halfway to Cape Town, becalmed by the side of the road just the other side of Bloemfontein.

At last this youngish guy called Jerry picked me up. He was an affable, well-educated sort of bloke, perhaps twenty or twenty-one years old, and we were quickly at ease with each other. Nevertheless, I sensed in him a sort of underlying bitterness which I couldn't quite trace to anything he'd told me about himself, which was admittedly not much. It was a pretty strong undercurrent, though, as if when his mind was in repose some pretty nasty subject was its natural resting place.

Sometime around two o'clock in the morning, it all came out. His hand gripped the wheel rather tightly as he went through the worst of it, with his knuckles showing up white in the light of the occasional oncoming headlights, and his voice seemed to drop an octave or two as he told the story.

He had been about fourteen years old when he found out he was adopted. Both his parents had sat him down on the family couch one warm sunny Sunday afternoon, and in very loving tones had calmly explained to him that after they'd been married ten years without being able to fall pregnant, they'd decided to adopt a baby, and he'd been the result. They'd loved him from the first, no worries about that, and when as so often happens, his mother had fallen naturally pregnant just a short time later, both parents were delighted but not at all regretful that they'd already adopted him. When his mother gave birth to his younger brother Joel, both parents knew that there would be no distinction between the two of them and that they would love *both* sons absolutely equally.

The reason they hadn't told him before this was simply that there had been no need. They didn't want any distinction to exist between the two brothers and, furthermore, they now lived in an entirely different part of the country to where Jerry and Joel had spent their first years. Neither parent had any living relatives, so there was no risk that anyone would tell him the truth of his origins and, besides, he really *was* their son, the way they loved him so—and they never had cause to think about the fact that he had started his life with them as an adoptee.

But now they'd decided they had to tell him of his beginnings because they had recently received word that Jerry's natural mother had been looking for him. Though they had done everything they could to keep her at a distance and had not co-operated one iota with her search for their whereabouts, even taking steps to keep it hidden, there was always a chance that she would break through and try to make contact with him. In case she succeeded, his parents said, they wanted him to hear the truth from them first and know all the reasons whey they'd kept it from him. More importantly, they wanted him to know how very deeply they loved him.

The whole time this was being recounted to him, Jerry had listened in a kind of daze, even as he focused on the sound of his brother Joel upstairs, practising over and over on his new electric guitar the first few chords of the famous 'Smoke on the Water' song: *bam bam bam, bam-bam, bam-bam, bam bam bam, bam bam . . .* and then his brother's wailing voice, '*Smoke on the waaaaaater, fi-uh in the sky . . .* !'

'. . . Jerry, are you listening?' his mother was asking him again, apparently for the third time. 'I said is there anything you'd like to say?'

No, Mum, not at all. Thank you for telling me. I know it's difficult for you, too, but all I need to know is that you love me as much as I love you and that's good enough for me.

Hugs and kisses all round, some tears from his mother and a firm handshake from his father and it was over. It was significant, he was to think later, that they never asked his opinion on whether or not *he* wanted to contact his natural mother, but he guessed their attitude was the right one. His mum and dad were his real parents, and this other woman just his mother biologically, which in comparison was nothing at all.

He talked about it with Joel later, of course, as the two talked about everything that happened to them, but Joel was an absolute brick about it.

'Don't be *reeee----dic----ulous*!' Joel had said, in that funnily broken way of speaking he had when he was really passionate about something, '*of coooourse* you're my *broth--er*—and I'm *yourrrr* brother. Who *cares* how we started out? We're *broth---errrsss* now, and always will *beeee*!!!'

Good ol' Joel.

A couple of years passed and nothing really changed substantially. In spite of himself, though, he'd occasionally find himself looking to see if he could detect any favouritism in his parents' treatment of Joel as opposed to him, but there really was nothing he could discern—except perhaps a slight sparkling in his father's eyes whenever Joel was around. His dad would also sparkle when he was around, too, of course; it just seemed a bit more intense with his younger brother, but that was probably because Joel had turned out to be so good at both cricket and rugby union, his dad's two favourite sports.

Jerry was not bad at those sports himself, mind, but he didn't hold the record for number of tries and runs scored in a season for his age-group the way Joel did. Nor was he meant to be 'the best-looking boy in school', the way they said Joel was, but Jerry knew he scrubbed up all right and didn't have any particular neuroses on that account. In the end, it was like Joel said: 'Who gives a daaaamn, Jerry?'

His natural mother never did succeed in getting through from wherever it was she was, and if he occasionally wondered about her, that was only normal he guessed.

Then, one day, when he was about seventeen and Joel sixteen, they'd had a fight. Nothing in particular, it had really just started as a muck-around wrestle in the bedroom which had turned only marginally more serious when his younger brother had accidentally poked him in the eye and Jerry had momentarily lost his temper. He'd meant to give Joel a semi-serious punch in the shoulder in reply, but at just the precise instant that he'd let fly, Joel had ducked into his fist and he'd connected with him full flush on the nose.

What happened next had been Jerry's waking point of departure every day since.

Joel dropped to the ground with a loud yelp, as blood gushed from his smashed nose, at the very same moment as his father had burst into the room. Their father looked first down at Joel's bloodied face, then up at Jerry standing over him with his fist still cocked, and then reacted with instantaneous fury.

Taking Jerry by the shoulders, he slammed him hard up against a cupboard, and with a slightly beery breath about two inches from Jerry's nose, had hissed out the next seven words in a voice shaking with rage.

'Don't you *ever* hit my son again.'

Then he turned on his heel, picked up Joel almost bodily and took him to the bathroom to get cleaned up.

Jerry had moved out a week later. There had been many tears from his mother, profuse apologies from his 'Father', and implorings from Joel not to be '*Stuuuup--id*', but there was no coming back from such a statement. He simply had to get out.

In the three years since, he'd shelved plans to go to university, and had instead spent the first year tracking down his natural mother. He'd succeeded, only to find that she'd died the previous year and in the two years since, he'd sort of bounced from job to job. He didn't have any long-term plans to speak of and the only thing he'd yet resolved was that he would never again live under his 'father's' roof.

And a mile up ahead was where he was going to have to leave me he was afraid, because there was a town about a hundred kilometres out to the west where he'd heard there was a chance he could get some work on surrounding farms.

We drove the last kilometre in silence and he left me by the side of the road with the dawn just starting to appear in the east. It looked like it was going to be a very cold, cloudy day.

The Day Jacques Blared His Horn

IT WAS WHEN I was living in the sleepy village of Donzenac, in the south of France . . . We knew something astounding had occurred even before Jacques got to us. The last time he'd blared his horn and thrashed the engine of his old van like that was . . . well, Jacques had *never* really done that before. By the time he'd squealed to a halt in front of the terrace of Madame Salesse's café, where we were all knocking back the last of our aperitifs before lunch, even old Monsieur Ducquet was awake and wondering.

'There's been *un hold-up* at the bank!' Jacques yelled gleefully, 'and Gendarme Columbo's *already* caught the bandit!'

Un *hold-up*!!! Our minds reeled. We looked at each other in stupefied wonderment. In our own sleepy village, on this normal, innocuous day, something . . . had . . . actually *happened*. It was unthinkable. It was unheard of. It was wonderful.

Excited almost beyond reason, we all crowded around Jacques to glean from him absolutely everything he knew. Which, as it turned out, was not much. Jacques had heard it from the butcher, who'd heard it from one of his customers, who'd heard it from sources unknown. The only thing that could be ascertained for sure was that there had been a hold-up and, somehow or other, Gendarme Columbo had played a major part in the criminal's apprehension. Columbo's role in the affair was almost as gratifying as the news itself.

As a regular of Madame Salesse's café, we knew Columbo well, and although a combination of his status as a young gendarme and his generally melancholic disposition had always prevented any real intimacy between us and him, I am sure we were the nearest thing he had to friends in the whole village.

But where was he? It was now twelve-thirty and there was still no sign of our friend, our knight, our hero.

Impatiently we waited. Time passed. More time passed and then, finally, at one-thirty, the door swung open and he was there. No bullfighter ever strutted into a roaring arena with more panache than Columbo swaggering into that café. Quite honestly, I barely recognised him. Gone were his usual hunched shoulders, his drawn, depressed look. Instead there was a sparkling, straight-backed fellow who looked for all the world as if he had just lived his finest hour. Which he had.

'*Well*!?!?,' we cried in unison.

'Can't say too much,' said Columbo. 'Official police business, you know.'

He continued with this line for about two more seconds before telling us the whole story.

At 11.03 am a man had walked into La Caisse D'Epargne bank and, finding only one female employee on duty and no clients, had pulled a gun. After emptying the register of 53 000 francs, he'd locked the woman employee in the toilets and scarpered. Only twenty seconds after he had left, she broke out and telephoned the gendarmerie.

A call went out on the radio alerting all units and reached Columbo at the bottom of Donzenac Hill, where he was about to nail someone for littering. As he was racing back up the hill, he passed a car careering down the other way and, had carefully noted down the registration number.

After hearing the woman's description of the gunman,

Columbo quickly traced the number to an address in the nearby town of Brive and at 11.35 am, the bandit was caught at the address, in the process of counting the loot.

Columbo was effusively congratulated by his superiors and, as I write, his photo is in the local papers. People are pointing him out as he walks down the street.

His explanation for his success, which he tells anyone that asks him at the café (and that is everybody), is a delight to hear:

'Il faut avoir le nez' he says, while tapping his nose and looking knowing. 'You've got to have the nose for this sort of thing.'

Ol' Columbo may never be the same again.

Little Dominique

JUST ON THE outskirts of Donzenac, on a quiet hillside overlooking the green valley below, she lies—in the family tomb, encircled by the other family tombs that make up Donzenac's cemetery. She has been there for the past twenty-five years, and to this day, the story of her life and death still weighs heavily on the spirits of some of the villagers. The roots of her death go back to a time before she was born, to the commencement of her parents' courtship.

Her father, Jean Salesse, was, as a young man, the best athlete of the whole region, with a particular talent for the villagers' beloved game of rugby. Extroverted, good looking, and a member of one of Donzenac's oldest and most illustrious families, he was the village beau. Her mother, Simone, a slim blue-eyed blonde, was held in nearly equal esteem in the nearby town of Varetz. But when it was announced that they were to be married, there was uproar in both villages. The couple were first cousins, and for the tribes of both Donzenac and Varetz this was an absolute taboo.

For weeks the villagers talked of the match, predicting all sorts of dire consequences if the young couple were to marry. Being young, French and in love, however, neither Jean nor Simone cared a fig for the bad talk and went ahead with the marriage.

Three years later their daughter, Dominique, was born. Disaster. She was born malformed in the extreme. She had no chin, buck teeth and a grossly protruding forehead and ears. More seriously, she also had a weak heart and a badly twisted spine, together with club feet. To compound all these problems, in the first flush of adolescence she was to grow a thick black down over her entire body, which, according to the villagers, made her look like a little monkey.

For all that, her brain was first-rate and when in accordance with Madame and Monsieur Salesse's wishes that she live a life that was as normal as possible, she went to school, she proved to be an excellent student. Though it might be expected that a little girl with such afflictions might be forced to suffer cruel playground jibes, by all accounts this never really happened. Perhaps it was because Madame Salesse always took great care to clothe and coiffure her child so as to hide her worst abnormalities. Or perhaps it was because the other children knew instinctively where to draw the line with taunting. Outside school hours Madame Salesse and Dominique were all but inseparable and they were a well-known sight together around and about Donzenac.

There are surely few sights more poignant than healthy parents promenading their badly stricken children, but in this case, when there was a known connection between the actions of the mother and the abnormality of the child, it must have been even more tragic than poignant.

Had all this happened in Hollywood instead of Donzenac, Dominique would no doubt be portrayed as an absolute angel, battling bravely against her terrible afflictions, but in reality it seems she had her foibles just like the rest of us. Oddly enough, 'vain and selfish' are words sometimes whispered about her and it seems she was not a little proud of her impeccable dress.

The only person of her own age Dominique was ever close to

was the now middle-aged Monique, who was for a time Dominique's best friend at school. The two were as close as close could be, right up until the age of thirteen when Monique first started taking an interest in boys. No sooner did Dominique sense this than she wrote a formal letter to Monique saying that she must make a choice between '*les garçons ou moi*'. Monique chose the garçons, and their friendship ended. Dominique continued at school alone.

At the age of fourteen Dominique went on her first excursion away from home, down to Barcelona in Spain, which lies about seven hours to the south of Donzenac. Three days after she had left, Madame and Monsieur Salesse were woken in the early hours of the morning by a phone call informing them that Dominique was dead. Her weak heart had simply stopped beating. At first light they set off for Barcelona, to bring their daughter's body home. Three days later they returned and Donzenac witnessed its most heavily attended funeral ever.

Two peculiarities stand out from the death rituals. Dominique was encased in a glass-topped coffin so everyone could see her (which is not the usual custom there), and though it was not known at the time, she had also undergone a special embalming process which was meant to preserve her body perfectly, so long as the process was repeated every ten years thereafter. In 1973 the tomb was reopened and Dominique's body was re-embalmed, though ten years later, in 1983, she was left in peace.

She lies there still.

Froggy Doggies

THE WHITECOATS HAVE all gone home, now. Finally, by the cold light of a wan French moon, I relate my story. I pray fervently that this manuscript will some day see the outside world.

It's about the froggy doggies. Poodles. There's beaucoup of them. There's très beaucoup of them. Oodles and oodles of poodles. Everywhere.

Always. In the fields. On the boulevards. In the restaurants. At the rugby matches. In the cafés. Sitting up like Jacky on the front seats of passing cars. Just everywhere.

I am not neurotic. Nor did I have an unhappy childhood. As a matter of fact, I used to like dogs. But, imagine living for four long years among a strange people who, essentially, possess only one brand of dog. One, just one, God help me.

And then, imagine that this one brand of dog, the poodle, is always following you, watching you. That no matter where you turn, what you do, where you go, there is always one more member of the poodle network. Staring at you. Wagging its stupid little tail. Yapping at you. Insolently. Incessantly.

Imagine all that, and you'll start to understand. It is more than True Blue flesh and blood can stand.

The first inkling I had of the seriousness of the situation was when the rugby club I play for here had a family picnic day to welcome me aboard. Needless to say, 'family' also meant dogs. The president and vice-president both had poodles. The treasurer and coach both had poodles. Of the fifteen players in first grade, no less than seven had poodles.

Right in the middle of the president's welcoming speech his poodle piddled on my leg.

'*Please* don't kick your poodle to death on my account, Monsieur le President,' I was about to plead magnanimously. 'It wasn't his fault.'

Only just in time, I noticed he hadn't missed a beat of his speech. Odd. Very odd. But things were to get even more bizarre.

I went out with a French girl, Michelle. Surprise, surprise, she had a poodle. 'Love me, love my dog,' she said. God knows I tried. But did she have to spend five hundred francs a month on taking it to poodle beauty salons, amongst other things? Did it have to sleep on the end of her bed at night in designer dog-pyjamas? And, worst of all, did Michelle have to keep three photos of the dog on her bedside table? Enough already.

I'd turn on the television. Ads for pet medical insurance, prominently featuring a poodle. 'Doesn't your little doggy deserve the very best medical care? Take out this insurance now . . .' I'd open a magazine. More poodle pictures. A story on this great new business that's just opened in Cagnes-sur-Mer. Basically, a lonely hearts match-making service for poodles. I'd go for a walk in town. Promenading poodles leaving omnipresent poodle-poo.

And on it went. My rugby team-mate Christian, whom I'd admired as the toughest man on earth, turned out to have had his poodle baptised. True, I swear it.

I'd go to a very classy restaurant. Froggy doggies every-where. *In* the restaurant, I mean. *At* the goddamn table, I mean. Truly. Sitting up on their owners' laps as they ate.

Over time I began to break down. I started seeing poodles

everywhere I looked. That wasn't necessarily a problem, though. It was when I started to turn into a poodle myself that I knew I was in trouble.

First, I started to grow fur on the palms of my hands. Then my feet began to turn into paws and my nose seemed always to be wet. I was always lying on my back and begging people to tickle my tummy.

Finally, they had to come and get me. Two enormous poodles in white coats, driving an ambulance. They took me back to this enormous white kennel, and that's where I am at the moment. If this manuscript ever gets out, at least you, my countryfolk, will know that it's not me, but this whole nation that is just crazy about poodles.

French Sex in the Park

FRIDAY, MIDNIGHT, AVENUE FOCH. Walking, walking, walking. L'Arc de Triomphe five hundred metres behind me. The Bois de Boulogne dead ahead. That's odd. Why are all those men waiting by the side of the road and looking at the traffic so expectantly? 'Excuse me, monsieur eighteen year old, just what are you expecting to come at you from out of that traffic?'

'Maybe a nice middle-aged woman will like the look of me, pull up and take me home for the night. This is where you stand if you want that to happen.'

Oh.

Walking. Walking. Why are these couples in cars pulled off by the side of the road? With their hazard lights flashing? Watching. Watching. The gentlemen from each of the cars are walking up and down along the line of cars, looking at the female occupants and having animated discussions with each other. 'Er, *excusez-moi*, monsieur well-dressed forty year old, what is this all about?'

'We are *les exchangistes*, the wife-swappers, and this is where you park your car if you wish to swap your wife for the night.'

Oh.

Walking. Walking. What are all those men around that car for? They look like enormous bees clustered around a giant piece of honeycomb. Rucking. Rucking. Rucking out the ol' Frenchmen. Finally, I can see what is in the car—four young ladies barely dressed at all. '*Excusez-moi, jeune mesdemoiselles*, what are you . . .?' No, on second thoughts, that's all right, I can see what you are doing.

They are, ah-hem, caressing each other in this car, on this busy avenue, with traffic everywhere and people all around, and I can see the Arc de Triomphe not a kilometre away. The steamy window rolls down.

'*Il est tellement **beau** celui-la*!' (He's so good looking, that one there!), one of them squeals, looking in my direction. Could it be, uh, *moi*, she is referring to? Could it . . .? Could . . .? It is not. It is the fellow in front of me. Would this young *garçon* care to go for a drive with them just up the road into the deep woods of the Bois de Boulogne, they want to know.

Would he ever.

Walking. Walking. Sheepishly walking away. 'What are you young men all hanging around this traffic circle for?'

'We are male prostitutes and our clients can drive around to get a good look at us before picking one of us up.' Oh.

Walking. Walking. Now into the Bois de Boulogne itself. The lights of the city recede and down the dirty boulevard I walk through the woods. Getting colder now. Traffic is light, which is just as well because the woods are so dark. Just up ahead there is a lone woman standing by the road with . . . with . . . clearly naked breasts above a miniskirt. When I am about fifty metres off, I see a fellow approach her, talk to her, and they then drop back together into the darkness of the woods. I can just see their outline behind some bushes about ten metres from the road. What the . . .? Surely she's not . . .? He's not *actually* . . .?

Yessum, they *are*.

Walking. Walking. Just around the corner in the maze of the woods there are more of them. They all look me up and down as I pass and hiss oddly in guttural voices. '*Cent francs . . . amour*', one hundred francs for . . . love. Cheap at the price. But that's funny, Little Red Riding Hood, they all have such deep voices, such big shoulders and such firm-looking breasts. They are practically naked, Mother.

When they walk, it is, as Bob Dylan would say, just like a woman . . . but vastly more pronounced. The window of a passing car rolls down and someone yells out '*Ç va les travelos*?' (How's it going, you transvestites?)

Oh, ma goodness. Oh, ma very goodness.

Sitting. Sitting. On a rock. Watching the transvestites in action, darting in and out of the woods with client after client, and chatting with them between stints as they smoke about two packets of my cigarettes. They're nearly all from Brazil and they're all . . . bolting into the woods in a blind panic. What's happening? It is the police in cars with flashing blue lights making what is apparently an extremely rare raid. Time to move on out of transvestite territory. Time, in fact, to think about getting a taxi to the airport for the early flight out. '*Excusez-moi*, monsieur le hot dog vendor, do you know how I can get out of the woods and to the nearest cab rank?'

'*Oui*, go straight up this road until you're out of the transvestite thicket and find yourself back among the real women prostitutes. Take a right there and walk about a hundred metres until you get to the S & M crowd with the whips and leather, et cetera. Just here you should see a boulevard leading off to the left and there should be a few cars parked by the side of the road with black men in them (for those whose particular turn-on is black men) and you should follow this road until you see a little avenue with lots of cars pulling in and out and lots of people standing around the cars . . . looking. This is where *les exhibitionistes* and *les voyeurs* get together. Walk straight ahead for a kilometre and you'll come to the cab rank.'

'Er, *merci*.'

Walking. Walking. It is exactly as he said, except for one small detail. He should have said, 'And then you'll come to this really young, beautiful and rather virginal-looking girl, dressed all in black, who'll ask you for a cigarette, and you'll chat for a few minutes with her, and you'll just be falling a little in love with her total charm and seeming innocence and you'll be thinking, "Surely *she's* not a prostitute, too", when she asks you if you'd care to take a turn behind yonder tree for a hundred francs. You'll decline, in order to think about it, shocked as you are, while she proceeds to go behind yonder tree with three clients in the space of fifteen minutes, and you'll feel like slitting your wrists. But, instead, you'll eventually just get up and walk away.'

Walking. Walking. Up to the taxi rank and out.

Barcelona

RUMOURS ABOUND THAT the Martian Academy for Advanced Space Cadets is soon to set aside an Earth People study afternoon for their students.

There can only be one place to send them. Right into the middle of the seamiest, most off-beamiest, square in all Barcelona—la Placa Reale—situated just off the Catalonian city's most famous thoroughfare, Las Ramblas.

There, not only would the young Martians pass almost unnoticed as they mingled with equally weird and wonderful looking Earth People, but more importantly, in the space of a single afternoon and evening they would be able to see a fair cross-section of the world's population passing by. Rich and poor, hippie and yuppie, Gucci shoes and bare feet—all traipse by in an unending procession from sun-up to moon-down, as the pigeons and palm trees sway. The plaza is a people-watching vista par excellence. At its very core—the people that most of the other people are watching—is a large group of resident ragamuffins of infinite variety, background and origin.

These are the ever-colourful Barcelona street people. The ones that would have been rounded up and repressed under the regime of General Franco, but who are now flourishing. You can tell the resident ragamuffins by their movements. While the tourists go round and round and the drifters go back and forth, the ragamuffins move slowly east, following the sun as it moves across the square. They live partly by petty crime, partly by cadging whatever they can from the tourists, and mostly on cheap red wine and sunshine.

Bob Dylan himself could have invented them. Real. Rainbowy. Ghost poets. Colourful, with each face a novel of past experience.

There is 70-year-old Carlos, the wrinkliest old man I have ever seen, bar none. The joke among the ragamuffins is that there is more skin on Carlos's face, because of the wrinkles, than on the rest of his body put together. It may just be true. Carlos stays alive by moving from table to table in the cafés that ring the square, and getting a few pesetas here and there. There is an old barefoot gypsy woman called Jana, who lives by the same method, though she precedes her demand for a handout by doing a frantic little gypsy song and dance routine. Hans, a tall drug-ridden German boy, also stands out. In the blazing heat he can be seen strutting across the square screaming out a very realistic imitation of Mick Jagger doing *Satisfaction*, pouting lips and all. My mate Elmo the car thief maintains that Hans is on the run from some drug bust in Munich, but Hans denies this saying he's already paid his dues to the German law.

Another well-known figure in the plaza is 'the bag lady'. Invariably dressed in something that looks like it has been made out of an old fertiliser bag, this woman goes from table to table in the cafés and asks for lumps of sugar. You give it to her, always expecting that she will then ask for money like everyone else, but she never does. What she does with the sugar no-one knows. To really get into a place like this one needs somewhere to stay. The best on offer is the Hotel Kabul, situated in the south-east corner of the plaza, right behind the part where the middle-aged prostitutes hang out.

Though called a hotel, it is in fact a collection of dormitories

situated on the first floor, right above a restaurant featuring fla-
menco dancers that go on late into the night, and right below
the aforementioned prostitutes' quarters. Fortunately, people
don't go to bed early at the Hotel Kabul, as the stereo effect from
above and below is awesome.

If this sounds like a low dive, you're right. The Ritz it ain't.
But whatever that indefinable quality is that makes low dives
into magical places, infinitely better than three-star hotels
(for backpackers at least), Hotel Kabul has it in spades. The usual
practice there is for guests to drink and smoke late into the
night, swapping travel stories and passionately discussing the
great questions of the day before finally going to bed and
sleeping late.

In the morning one follows the sun as it travels across the
plaza, perhaps hanging out with the ragamuffins, and then at
night one discusses once again the great questions of the day
until the wee hours. While certainly not for everybody, it's hog
heaven for those of us that like that sort of thing. The hotel
offers all the pleasures of what I imagine communal living
must be, without having to shave your head and wear
orange robes.

The first time I stayed there (I've since been back three
times), six of us became so close that two days before we
were to be scattered, we talked late into the drunken night
about the possibility of holding a reunion. The thought was to
meet 20 years exactly from that date, on the first floor of
whatever building might be standing where the Hotel Kabul
now was, and that no matter where we all were, or what we
might be doing, we would all make the effort to come.
Further, it was decided that if any one of us were to become fab-
ulously rich they were to pay for the ones that might find
themselves financially strapped.

Of course, in the sober light of day we changed our minds
and decided to hold the reunion that evening on the other side
of the plaza (it would be cheaper to make the trip and we
knew we could all make it), but somehow or other the links
that were forged between us then still exist now, three years
on—with odd postcards, letters and phone calls coming and
going. It was in fact at this reunion the following night that an

Driving in Beirut

SURE THERE ARE road rules in Beirut. It's just that they're not obvious on first glance, that's all. At least they can be learned with only a little close scrutiny. First, however, you've got to understand something about the territory . . .

In view of a recent report in *The Guardian* that the Baghdadis were increasingly running red lights as the Gulf War approached—it simply didn't matter any more—it's hardly surprising that sixteen years of civil war in Lebanon should have had the same effect, only infinitely magnified. But it's not total anarchy. Understandings have evolved which substitute as *de facto* rules. The Beirutis know, for example, one should try to keep on the right-hand side of the road. More or less, with many exceptions, such as you don't feel like it.

For the rest, let us look briefly at a few of the other 'understandings'.

- *Right of way*: Goes generally to that vehicle which both drivers subconsciously know will come off better in a crash. If I

91

have an old Volkswagen and you have an old Mercedes, then you have right of way. There is, of course, an exception. If I have deliberately plastered concrete all over my VW, as cheap protection against rust or mortar fire or both, and you have only a normal Mercedes, I get right of way. Why? Because I couldn't give a cup of warm camel's spit if I take a few more dings in my vehicle; you, on the other hand, do. My car should have formed part of an artificial reef long ago—so do your worst, boyo, I'm coming through. Get the drift? Generally, trucks trump cars, and tanks trump everybody.

- *Speed*: Whatever you can manage. On the open road you can fang it without fear or favour from anybody other than the guys manning roadblocks, where it is best to come to a dead halt of your own volition. In the city it is more cluttered, but people keep the pedal to the metal, anyway, for a very good reason: car bombs are still in vogue and the common wisdom is that the faster you move past parked cars the less chance you have of being blown up. Truly.

- *Road signs*: These mean nothing at all, though many still exist. 'No Entry' means 'Lead on, Macduff'. 'Dead End' means that when the war started there was something blocking the way at the end of the street, but who is to say if it still exists now? Drive on. In fact, only one road sign has any effect on the populace—'No Parking' signs. These are obeyed totally. Not because of the signs themselves, so much as what has been done with the iron bars they were perched on. These have been cut into three pieces and welded together into a tepee-like structure, about a half-metre high—with three cruel prongs pointing outwards. Strategically placed on the roadside where you don't want people to park—in front of your shop, for instance—they form a very effective argument.

- *Pedestrians*: As a general rule, pedestrians have no rights at all, unless they carry machine guns, when they have *lots* of rights. Plenty of pedestrians actually do carry guns and they are given a wide berth. Then again, if your vehicle happens to be a tank or jeep with a machine gun, you take precedence.

So far, so good? Car trumps pedestrian. Pedestrian with gun trumps car. Car with gun trumps pedestrian with gun. Now the next, most crucial step. Pedestrian with the gun and red beret trumps everybody and everything—even if you're driving the Opera House on wheels and have the guns of Navarone aboard.

See, the red beret identifies the pedestrian as a soldier of the Syrian occupation force. It is not only a good idea to give him right of way but proper road etiquette says that if he asks, you should give his boots a bit of a spit and polish as well. It's not just that in a town full of bad dudes, the Syrians are reputedly the baddest of them all; it's that in a town of fractured factions themselves factionalised, the Syrians are the only cohesive unit . . . and if you damage one Syrian, you answer to them all.

But to the car itself. The main thing, indeed the only thing, is that it goes. There are no official requirements for roadworthiness in Beirut and when getting your car ready for the road you can forget such ancillary accoutrements as blinkers, wipers, rearview mirrors, et cetera.

The only accoutrement that counts is the horn, and this had better be good. You see, in Beirut, the horn works in reverse. One does not occasionally lean on the horn to let someone know you are there. Instead, one occasionally takes one's hand off the horn so as to stun people with the momentary silence. At least, that's the only reason I can think of, because the rest of the time everybody circles around with one hand on the wheel and one hand on the horn. Really.

Just one last thing. If ever you come through Beirut on a cycling trip, be advised: though it is not compulsory for you to wear a helmet, it would probably be a very good idea.

Travel

IT'S ONE OF THOSE ideas that could only come out of California—an entrepreneur has just released a cassette entitled *Thirty Classics in Thirty Minutes*.

True. You want to appear well read? You've come to the right place. Instead of spending a month ploughing your way through the whole *War and Peace* saga (boooring) you just listen to a one-minute summation of the plot on the tape and will forever more be able to drop with ease at the dinner party little ice-cubes of knowledge which imply an iceberg of literary erudition that doesn't really exist—but no-one will be the wiser.

I hate to say it, but all up I think it's an idea which has great merit and enormous potential. I'm sure the whole concept can be expanded into other areas.

Like travel for example . . . why drag your bod in and out of the world's airports, losing your baggage, getting ripped off by taxi drivers, pickpocketed by thieves, all the while catching all kinds of exotic diseases and spending money like it was just so much Monopoly cash—all so you can have the appearance of being well travelled and worldly wise? Why not memorise those few key points and telling details that bona fide world travellers all know, and then be able to stay at home in the comfort of your loungeroom?

Listen up:

India

The gist: You'd no sooner landed at Bombay than you came down with a bad case of 'India shock', the famed condition of new arrivals from the West who become so disoriented by the weirdness of the teeming masses that for a couple of days it feels like they're living in someone else's slo-mo dream. But you recover and discover amid all the appalling poverty and over-crowdedness a people who have risen above their material circumstances to live lives that seem so spiritually full as to make ours seem embarrassingly superficial by comparison.

The telling detail: Who can ever forget the albino Indian bloke who hangs around outside Bombay's Taj Mahal Hotel offering to wash cars for a couple of rupees? Wasn't it weird how he was blond enough to look like a small, squinty kind of Swede, yet was really as Indian at Mahatma Gandhi and hot curry rolled into one?

And the *really* weird thing was when he'd sit with his brother on the pavement, having lunch beneath the midday sun. Both of them would ask you for a bit of '*baksheesh baba*' as you passed, and though they were obviously as close as brothers could be, you'd always reflected how weird it was that two such disparate-looking men had sucked on the same mother's breast.

Nepal

The gist: You first became interested in going there after hearing for the hundreth time Bob Seger's song '*K..K..K..K.. K..K..Kathmandu*', and seeing you were in India, anyway, what the hell?

And you're *soooo* glad you did. After all the crush and heat of the teeming humanity in India, it was such an unspeakable pleasure to get to the open spaces and friendly people of Nepal. And for the first time in your life, you know what it must be like to be rich, because for a mere five American dollars you can eat the best meal God ever gave in one of Kathmandu's many terrific restaurants—so, naturally, you ate at restaurants three times a day.

The telling detail: You were appalled to meet, as all visiting Australians do, the forty-something-year-old Australian by the name of 'Jed' who hangs out on the famed Freak Street, looking for anyone speaking with our broad vowel sounds, just so he can cadge some money from them. Basically, the guy is what they call 'drug-fu----'; he first came to the place in the early seventies as a bright-eyed twenty-one-year-old tourist, got caught up in smoking marija-hoochy at give-away prices, went mainlining from there, and soon committed the ultimately stupid act of selling his passport for fifty bucks and has been there ever since in a perpetual cloud of dope smoke.

You don't know if it's just part of his act or not, but he asks all Australians he meets if they know a Mrs Carlow from Brisbane because that's his mum and he often wonders how she's getting on, and by the way can you spare a couple of bucks?

Egypt

The gist: All the tourist brochures talk about Cairo as being the city that has 'the gentle blending of East and West', but as far as you could see it had all the gentle blending of a front-on car smash. You mean it! Is that city chaos or what? When you're out on the streets it's like standing just outside the gates of the Sydney Cricket Ground when they open the gates at the end of a day, except these people were going in a dozen different directions at once.

Sure the King Tut display at the Egypt Museum is impressive, but hell, it'd *want* to be, seeing as it took you three hours to get there in the first place—from a hotel, that was, after all, only a couple of kilometres away.

The telling detail: Those doors on the Cairo Hilton. Could you believe it? Like every other low-rent tourist, you occasionally like to buy some high-rent breakfast in a swish hotel just to get back into a little bit of Western civilisation, and every time it's that same thing. You quicken your pace those last few steps to get into all that air-conditioned coolness and instead of opening inwards, like *every other automatic hotel door in the world*, it opens outwards and keeps hitting you on the noggin.

Argentina

The gist: So now you know what Paul Keating meant with all his talk of a 'Banana Republic'. Everywhere you go, there is a sense of a once-grand country now in serious decay—marvellous edifices all crumbling, the wide boulevards in desperate need of renewal, the hot tap blowing cold air and the cold tap blowing nothing . . . and so on.

The people, for all that, are extremely hospitable if you know them and at the very least friendly if you don't. You know it sounds sexist to say it, or politically incorrect or something, but the women are so extraordinarily beautiful you can't understand how it's quite possible without cosmetic surgery being built into their health insurance.

The telling detail: The extraordinary wealth apparent on Calle Florida in Buenos Aires. Kind of an Argentinian version of Los Angeles' Rodeo Drive, this street caters exclusively to people who could afford to buy Tasmania as a holiday island and yet it is plastered with beggars who are hoping for the odd alms for the poor.

Hong Kong

The gist: Take one island and turn it into one big air-conditioned shopping mall. Turn up the heat to almost unbearable levels on the outside so that the only way for any visitors to survive is by going shopping. Further punish any deviation from the plan of shopping till you drop by making sure that each and every road over the whole island is permanently clogged with chockablock traffic. Fool tourists into thinking they're getting a good deal while there by offering truly absurd prices for tennis racquets, shoes, cameras, TV sets et al, but absolutely PUNISH them on everything else—from hotel rooms to telephone calls to meal prices. One way or another, make sure that no-one leaves the island with more than a single brass razoo left in their pocket.

The telling detail. The square just outside the downtown Hilton Hotel which every Sunday, all day, is completely full of *Ahmas*, the Hong Kong Chinese word for maids/nannies.

Mostly Filipinos, they gather there in little groups of half-dozen and talk and giggle from sun-up to sun-down about their masters and mistresses and news of their family at home. When you talk to them they are extremely friendly and seem quite happy with their lot. They mention in passing what they are getting paid per week for their sixteen-hour days, and though you are entirely appalled at such a scant fee, they rejoin that while it might sound like little enough to rich tourists, it's still three times more than what they would be getting for the same work at home.

Paris

The gist: Fantastic. From the street life to the architecture, from the cuisine to the fashion, it's just about the most knock-out city you've ever been in, pulsating with life and vitality for the full 24 hours of the day. The truly amazing thing about this city which everyone raves about, is that it really *is* very good. Expensive, yes; difficult to navigate your way around, absolutely; but surely it is the city Jesus would choose to make his comeback in if he was feeling like a change from the Middle East.

The telling detail. You can spot all the newly arrived tourists from across the Channel, by the way they charge down the Champs Elysees on the *left*-hand side of the pavement, bumping into people all the way. The French follow the international rule of thumb, of walking on the same side of the pavement that they drive on the road—which is to say on the right—and though the visiting English invariably get the hang of that after a day or so, those just off the boat make very heavy weather of it, proceeding upstream against the oncoming human tide.

Drugged and Drunk and On the Typewriter

THERE'S THIS GREAT American writer called Hunter S. Thompson, see, and what he does is get himself tanked up on whisky and all kinds of stuff and wait till three a m when he comes in off the porch, where he has been sitting nude while shooting his six-gun into the wilderness, and then he just writes down what comes into his head. He breaks all the normal rules of grammar and syntax and writing, but, somehow, what he comes up with is invariably very readable and sometimes brilliant or, at the very least, it's different.

And if the rest of us can't write like him, at least we can mimic his actions and see what comes out. So, half a bottle of whisky behind me, and forty shots fired into the low hills of Annandale, let us turn our nude and drunken attention to sport and see what happens . . .

Yeah, and what the hell is it with these soccer people? If the really conservative boffins who run rugby can somehow get their act together long enough to change the rules of rugby for the better, why can't the soccer people do the same?

Isn't it obvious to the administrators that these days it's pretty darn difficult for the players to score, and so often so deadly boring for us to watch, when *maybe if they widened the goals* (I know, I know, I'm a genius) it would make it more difficult for the goalie to defend . . . and there would be more goals scored . . . and the whole thing would be far more interesting . . . and what do you think?

I mean, do you think that maybe the people that riot at soccer matches all over the world *are trying to tell us something*? Like they're so bored, they'd rather crack someone over the head than endure it a single moment longer?

And I know I'm repeating myself, but I am drunk, and it works for Hunter S. and it works for Jeffrey Bernard, so maybe it'll work for me . . . but the goals are pretty much as wide now as when they invented and formalised the damn game, but the goalies, you see, are now far more athletic and can now leap at least twice as fast to the left or right as Bob Beamon used to do in the long jump, so what is the point of even shooting at the goal, because the boogers are just too damn good . . . and why haven't I been made a soccer writer yet, when I seem to know so damn much on the subject?

And tennis. One more tennis game and I swear I'll puke. It used to be interesting, didn't it? Like you'd even have a fair idea at any given moment of who were the top ten players in the world. But now it just bores me rigid and the only one I know anything at all about is Andre Agassi and I only know *him* because I always rather fancy I'd like to give him a good smack in the mouth.

And there's another guy called Jakob Hlasek, I think, and he is ninth in the world or something, last I heard, and nobody knows or cares anything about him, except his mum, I guess, and how can tennis be in a healthy state if a guy called Jakob Hlasek from Switzerland is currently one of the nine best players on the planet and nobody knows the first damn thing about him? I ask you.

And boxing. I know boxing is brutal and there is a worldwide move to ban it and those forces seem to be gaining ground and really, intellectually, there's just about no argument you can

make against them, except the truth of the matter loosened up by whisky.

The sight of two full-grown men going hard at it in a fight to the canvas is just about the most spectacular and gripping thing you can see in sport, for a lot of us, anyway. See, I think it must be its very awfulness which provides its incredible magnetism. We hate ourselves for loving it, but love it anyway.

And rugby. How come I'm now thirty years old and never been able to touch my toes or do any of those stretching exercises that all rugby coaches insist on these days and I've still never been injured by pulling a muscle and yet all these young bucks are coming up through the ranks who are so well versed in all the tenets of techno-rugby, who can touch their toes with their *elbows* if they want, and use all the new-fangled terms like 'marmalade jam', 'carbohydrates', and 'hamstrings'? Yet these guys, I say, these guys get injured all the time. I swear they do. Could there be some cosmic paradox at work here, when the more you know about the way your body works, and the more dedicated you are about taking infinitely delicate care of it, the more likely you are to injure the brute?

And while we're on the subject, not that we really are, what happened to all those wonderful things they used to say about basketball? Has that game gone off the boil something serious or what? When the basketball troops used to extrapolate their crowd figures to the mid-nineties they reckoned that there'd be a pensioner couple in lower Woop-Woop with a crook car and a sick dog who might stay home one Saturday night, but just about all the rest of Australia would be at the basketball. And it hasn't happened.

And how come we like watching Rugby League on the box so much when basically we're seeing the same action—guy takes the ball up, gets belted, falls over, guy takes the ball up, gets belted, falls over—about *ten thousand* times in eighty minutes? Doesn't anything else happen in that game? I ask you.

And child birth. I wonder if it's true what Mary Decker once told me (*Mary and I? Hell, yes, best of friends*), that her ability to train intensely in running had been improved since she had given birth to her child, quite simply because her pain threshold had been heightened so much that she knew that her body could stand a lot more pain than she had been previously putting it through.

And damn bad about sport and business, isn't it? I mean, it really gives me the raging pips. In the old days sport was sport, business was business and ne'er the Mark Twain did meet—these days it's everywhere, and everybody seems to be making a buck out of sport everywhere you look. And try this for a theory: you know how sometimes you see on the television slow-mo shots of kids with Down's Syndrome running in a 100 metre race and you've only got to look at it for about three seconds before the hairs on the back of your neck rise and you're feeling all choked up? Maybe that's because the only place sport is absolutely pure any more—without sponsorship, drugs, nastiness, extreme competitiveness et cetera—is in races like that. And suddenly I'm feeling like I might have had a bit too much whisky and my head is feeling heavier and heavier and hea . . .

tyyyu

jhkkkkk

nnjhkkkk

uutuuuu

. . . uuuuuuuuuuuuuuuuuuuuuuuuuuuh where were we? Who am I? And one more thing that springs to this sozzled mind is that I keep reading about you English people raving about the fellow they've got over there who is the head of the Manchester Olympic bid and how he alone has moved Manchester ahead on the hit parade blah, blah, blah.

Listen to me. You want to know what dedicated is? I'll tell you what dedicated is. Dedicated is the guy we've got as head of the Sydney Olympic bid, a bloke by the name of Rod McGeoch. How dedicated is he? He's *sooooo* dedicated that, get this, he made a supreme self-sacrifice to beat all self-sacrifices when Juan Antonio Samaranch was in town recently. Juan Antonio had been trucked around to all the possible Olympic sites with the usual rose petals scattered before him wher-

ever he went, when, late in the afternoon, he was taken by boat across Sydney Harbour to meet the Prime Minister at his magnificent habourside residence, Kirribilli House.

McGeoch and Juan Antonio had just alighted from the boat and were walking up the lawn to meet the Prime Minister, who awaited with his hand outstretched, when McGeoch saw it, right ahead of them . . . a fairly large dollop of Prime Ministerial doggie-do right in the way of the Olympic kingpin. McGeoch tried to steer him gently away, but to no avail. The most powerful man in the Olympic movement and the doggie-do were on a direct collision course. The fate of Sydney's Olympic bid hung in the balance. There was only one thing to do.

McGeoch skipped half a pace forward and trod directly in it himself. Greater love for his country hath no man than this. 'All in a day's work,' McGeoch was heard to mutter soon afterwards. And that's the sort of guy he is. That's what *true* dedication is and if you're reading this, Juan Antonio, I mean Mr Samaranch, I mean your Holiness, I mean *your Royal Bees-knees-ed-ness*, I would just like to ask you to remember when the voting time comes around who exactly it was that stepped in the doggie-do for you, the guy from Manchester or the guy from Sydney?

And I wonder if humans are the only animals that have organised sports. If the monkeys or dolphins have games that they play which we just can't discern. It would certainly be interesting to know, but rather hard to find out, I suppose.

I suppose. I suppose. I suppose. I don't suppose this formula for an article is wearing a bit thin is it? Well let's stop it there.

Stop it there. Stop it there, there, there, it can only get better.

Waiter! More whisky.

A Fistful of Dollies

I LOVE DOLLS. Even now. Dunno why. Maybe because I never got a chance to grow tired of them like my sister did. Maybe because she always got to stay inside by the fire to cuddle and dress them, while I had to go outside to chop the wood, fetch the water, pick the oranges and feed the dog. To me, dolls came to represent *looxury*.

The truly wonderful thing for all us doll fetishists is that we are now awash in doll news as never before. See, as far as international events go, you can keep your earthquakes and your plagues and your crumbling communist empires, my friends and I are only interested in such things insofar as they affect dolls.

Why, not so long ago a story appeared in the paper which created quite a stir among the guys I can tell you. It was about Barbie dolls selling well in Moscow. Well, we never. In a country where the base monthly income is 2500 roubles (A$33), the guys just couldn't believe that they'd bother trying to sell any doll that cost 1900 roubles ($A25).

The thing is, most of us are already in love with the Russian version of Barbie, called Veronika. She's our real pin-up doll. So different from Barbie, so . . . so . . . down-home and approachable. Veronika isn't drop-dead gorgeous, doesn't have glamorous clothes, doesn't come with exotic accoutrements such as surfboards or hairdryers—or anything at all. She's just a nice, normal girl; the way we like it. And besides, Veronika is so cuddly—bigger and softer than Barbie, without being lumpy and shapeless like the dolls the commies used to turn out.

We know what you're thinking—you're thinking how very odd that grown men should know so much and care so deeply about dolls and it's probably all a front for the fact that they're really into the blow-up variety. Not at all. In fact, we *detest* such vulgarity, such cheapening of the doll ethos through nasty sex.

The only lifelike dolls we're interested in, and then simply as a partner for some of our female dolls, are the Ideal Man dolls, marketed successfully in the United States recently by the Anatomical Chart Co in the town of Skokie, Illinois, for $39.95. (Me and the guys love arcane doll details like that.)

Dressed in coat and tie, the Ideal Man doll says what women are *apparently* waiting to hear. At the press of a button, he chants the following phrases: 'I respect your career.' 'You cook wonderfully.' 'How about a nice massage?' 'You relax and I'll do the dishes.' 'You inspire me.' Or, 'let me hold you. I need your warmth.' And, 'Your smile makes my day.'

You think we're making this up—but we're not. It's all true. Just as we're not making up the fact that in Japan they've recently had marvellous success with their 'I am sorry doll', which is for harassed managers to scream at. There are three basic versions of this doll—the boss, the wife and the woman police officer—all of whom can be made to gurgle, 'Please forgive me', as you hurl abuse at them. Yes, even the guys and I think this a bit odd, and over-the-top even for us.

The great hit of the moment in the doll world is Judy, the Mommy-to-be Doll. We love her, too. What a little wonder—pop-on pregnant stomach with a little baby doll in her belly.

Judy can have babies all week long without changing her smile or taking her wedding ring off.

You can get a partner Charlie doll if you like, but the guys don't like Charlie. Not good enough for our Judy, they say. A few keep Judy just for themselves, but most of us don't feel quite up to that just yet and put Judy with the Ideal Man doll—not for our pleasure, you must understand, but for Judy's. We love her. Simple as that.

It is a far, far better thing we do, than we have ever done; it is a far, far better rest we go to, than we have ever known.

Botham is a 'Convict' Deep Down

OH YES, MR BOTHAM, such a very nice, nice thing to say.

'What could be better than to beat the Aussies in Melbourne, playing in front of 100,000 convicts,' the great man said, referring to the prospect of playing against Australia at the Melbourne Cricket Ground as part of the cricket World Cup.

Apparently, His Nibs' remark was greeted with wide applause by you lot in the Mother Country. Or at least that's the way we hear it.

And there you Poms go again. Looking down your long noses at we poor colonials. Reminiscent of the aristocratic New Yorker who once famously said, 'My dear, if you're not living in New York, you're really just camping out . . .', you Englanders seem to think you are living on the bellybutton of the world. All of which is particularly galling for those of us who really are living there, we Sydney-siders. Most especially when it comes to matters of sport.

Let's go over a few little home truths here, shall we?

First the good news. In the history of sport, no-one has been more inventive than you Brits. Practically every international sport worth speaking of—with the exception of basketball—was invented on your once-secluded island. Probably because you had nothing better to do, but that's another story. From tennis, golf, rugby, football, badminton, competitive sailing, through competitive cycling, lawn bowls and a couple of hundred others that I can't think of right now, you thought of them, refined them and, when it first came to international competitions, dominated them.

But now for the bad news. (Hold still, now, this is going to hurt me more than it does you.) You've lost the plot, haven't you? You can't win them any more, can you? At least, not regularly.

Noah had just thrown away his gumboots the last time one of yours won Wimbledon. And will you tell me again, Grandpa, about the time when the English cricket team were considered the best on the planet?

Believe me when I say that I don't want to use that maddening condescension usually reserved for the English when talking to their poor colonial cousin Australians, but, the thing is . . . while you're currently not doing too badly at cricket or rugby, it's not as if you're world champions or anything, is it? As a matter of fact, *we* are . . . we Australians, you know?

And in the silent watch of the night, when you're lying on your backs and staring at the cracks in the ceiling, surely you must wonder how come every time you set foot on an international sporting field there is one Australian—or two, or eleven or fifteen—waiting there ready to rip your arms off and beat you around your heads with the bloody stumps? Come, come now. Of course you have.

The reason we are able to so summarily dispense with you is a very simple one, whether you've discovered it or not. Mr Botham was perhaps making passing reference to it when he mentioned convicts.

See . . . way, way back in the dark past ages, many many of your great-great-great-grandpappies were being mean and nasty and downright awful to our similarly far-back fore-bears. And this is where the factor of the get-up-and-go chromosomes started to kick in. All of our ancestors with these said chromosomes simply got up and went.

Either of their own volition, as in saying 'the hell with it' and heading off to Australia or the United States as emigrants, or by committing some truly heinous crime against the establishment, like stealing a chicken or a mouldy piece of bread. In which case they were soon caught and transported to Australia for perpetuity. Over time, the inevitable happened. Your gene-pool of get-up-and-go chromosomes was inevitably weakened to a very, very thin gruel, while in Australia ours started to positively bubble with the stuff.

You've seen the result now, haven't you? Two hundred years later, when it comes to get-up-and-go, you people must make do with the new descendants of the very few people with get-up-and-go who didn't get caught stealing chickens—like Botham himself—while in Australia we *only* breed people with get-up-and-go.

Here, my friends, is your problem, on the sporting field. With such a weak gene-pool, your only way forward is à la Geoffrey Boycott—a stolid, solid, steady-as-she-goes 'two degrees to port, if you please, Mr Briggs'—while we Australians are the only ones capable of a 'damn the torpedoes, full speed ahead' point of view.

Do you get it? Your get-up-and-go reserves are so severely depleted that you're essentially a nation of Boycotts, while Australia is populated by Bothams. Now the fact that Mr Botham—one of ours spiritually, if not on his passport—should so publicly insult us worries us not that much. Rather, we take such irreverence for correct form, just another sign that he should have been born in Australia.

But regardless, we're going to rip his arms off anyway and go through the whole 'bloody stump' thing, slowly, just for the slight on our honour.

We're like that, we convicts.

Auckland

I HEARD RECENTLY that Phil Scarr is back to eating solids again, which is great. If only I wasn't still haunted by the memory of what caused his many medical afflictions in the first place . . .

He was playing his first big representative game, on the wing for New South Wales against the mighty 1990 Auckland side at Eden Park.

I was in the same side, and about mid-way through the first half we were taking such a drubbing from the swarming hordes of Aucklanders that I decided not only that something had to be done but also that I was just the man for the job.

Thus, entirely ignoring our halfback Nick Farr-Jones, who was so screaming for the ball it seemed his tonsils might very possibly fall out, I rolled from the back of the maul with every honest intention of heading upfield, taking the battle right into the teeth of those dastardly Aucklanders.

But . . . on *second* thoughts, maybe it would be better to head across field instead. The Auckland forwards still looked a bit willing for more, and I thought there might be a break in the traffic a bit further out, where I could do *even more* damage to the brutes.

Nothing. No break. Just huge Aucklanders coming down hard from everywhere. I kept running straight across field regardless, all the while dummying as if I might pass to one of my own backs—to confuse the defence, like.

Presently, though, there was only one of my backs left that I could possibly unload the ball to and that was Phil Scarr, out there on the wing, and . . . and . . . what was that? He was trying to *signal* something to me. What did he mean by shaking his head and waving his arms around in front of his body like that? Did he mean he, in fact, didn't *want* me to pass the ball to him? Well, I never . . .

It was just about then that, out of the corner of my eye, I spied the extremely formidable figure of Scarr's opposing winger, Va'aiga Tuigamala, fully launched, all 110 kilograms of him, and heading straight for us.

Admittedly it's not much to have on your rugby tombstone —'*FitzSimons once delivered one of the great hospital passes of the modern age*'—but there didn't seem like a lot else that I could do. It was either the young 'un or me. I decided to give Phil the pass, even as Tuigamala tracked the ball and made his own commitment.

Even now I think if I hadn't got the ball into Scarr's hands in the absolute nick of time, the fearsome Auckland winger would surely have been sent off and spent a long time suspended—because, as it turned out, he was totally committed to the tackle even before the ball got to Phil. And I also think, in passing, that in the long and glorious rugby career of Tuigamala, it probably still stands alone as one of the most devastating tackles he ever made.

Whatever, somewhere between one-hundredth and two-hundredths of a second after I got the ball into Scarr's hands, 'Inga the Winger' hit him like an exploding torpedo in the chest, with a force that rattled even *my* teeth and, when the smoke had cleared, all we could see was Scarr's left foot coming out at rather an odd angle from beneath Inga's body. The Aucklander then slowly got up, a little shaken himself with the force of his own tackle, and we all looked down aghast to see if there possibly could be any survivors from such a hit.

There were, but only just.

Sorry about that, Phil.

Anyway, as I said, he's now back on solids and is apparently doing quite well, so that's the main thing, what? 'Forgive and forget'—that's what I always say.

And, I dunno, it was always a bit like that for me against Auckland. Things always seemed to go wrong.

Like the very first game I played against them, in 1984. Again it was at Eden Park, and on this occasion my direct opponent in the lineout was that greatest of all great second-rowers, Andy Haden. Not that I was impressed or anything, mind. In fact, from memory I think I announced to all and sundry that come the end of the game I fully intended to be hanging Haden's scalp from the string of my shorts.

And it very nearly happened, damn nearly, in fact. The first lineout of the game was our throw-in and, praise the Lord and pass the ammo, our captain signalled that the ball was to be thrown to me. Using our top-secret code, I indicated to our hooker, Lance Walker, that I wanted a lob ball. And Lance, in fact, threw one that looked exactly like the Sydney Harbour Bridge, which is to say perfect.

That poor goose Haden swallowed my feint forward, effectively taking him out of the play as he'd hurled his own body forward, and after a quick step back I soared towards the heavens confident as all get-out.

And, YESSSSSSS! Right into my hands. I pulled it down, knowing that I already had both hands not only on the ball, but probably the man-of-the-match award as well. Then I took the textbook position with the ball still in hand as I made ready to give the ball to Farr-Jones and also give all the photographers plenty of time to get good shots.

Then it was like one of those surreal slow-mo scenes you see in the movies sometimes. I was just about to at last give the ball to Farr-Jones when what do I see? I see a big hand appear, coming from between my legs, coming up at the ball, and then—ally-oop!—giving the ball the most gentle of slaps. I was entirely powerless to stop it, and was obliged to watch the ball sail back over my shoulder, perfectly into the hands of the Auckland halfback who sent his own backs away for a try.

That proved to be the highlight of my game against Haden, as after that it was all downhill. The worst part was having my own scalp bounce against his knobbly knees as he walked off at the end of the game. Lord I hated that.

Even when playing for Australia against Auckland later that year, things were still jinxed. It wasn't just that I gave away three silly penalties in the second half. I could have lived with that.

It was that Grant Fox kicked all three of them from an absurdly long range and we ended up losing by nine points— even as my Wallaby career started slowly sinking in the west.

Anyway, you get the drift.

I'm not saying that I actually want New South Wales to 'moider da bums' or anything, but what I am saying is that I think a score of about 60-0 is necessary to avenge just the wrongs that Auckland have done to me alone over the past ten years.

Importance of Being an Artful Competitor

YOUR HONOUR, I OBJECT. How many times are those of us with features broken-nosed and cauliflower-eared going to have to encounter the automatic assumption that we are also of rough mind? For there it was again the other day, yet another story about the surprising intelligence and refinement of a particular star of a contact sport. Why should such a thing be even worthy of comment, dammit?

Every time, it's the same basic theme dressed up a dozen different ways, about how such-and-such rugby player/boxer/basketballer/wrestler may be rough and tough in the sporting arena, may be the sort of man to dine on bolts for breakfast and lampposts for lunch, but when away from it, he really likes to listen to music/go to art shows and even read books.

I put it to you, sir, that the wellspring of such condescending stories seems to be an amazement whenever the world of rough sport and the world of the arts and intelligent thought overlap.

Arts people have often been just as guilty, looking down their noses at 'sweaty, Neanderthal rugby players' and assuming that boxers have to be monosyllabic, if not, indeed, demi-syllabic. In our defence, we Neanderthals should like to place before the court the likes of the most celebrated aesthete of all, Oscar Wilde, to show the two worlds are not incompatible.

Although Wilde later cultivated the image of a dandy well above sports—'I'm afraid I play no outdoor games at all . . . except dominoes . . . I have sometimes played dominoes outside French cafés'—he had another side. Not only did Wilde not mind watching sport now and then, but at a strapping 190 centimetres he was also into it himself. His favourite sport was, of all things, boxing. And not always with gloves on.

In Richard Ellman's excellent biography of Wilde, there is even a story recording the scene of Wilde as an eighteen year old, reading one of his poems to his class at school in Dublin, when one of the bullies sneered in derision.

'Wilde went up to him and asked him by what right he did so,' Ellman records. 'The [bully] laughed again, and Wilde struck him in the face. Soon everyone was outside and the two antagonists squared off. No-one gave Wilde a chance, but to general astonishment he proved to have a devastating punch and utterly worsted his opponent.'

When Wilde went up to Oxford and settled into Magdalen College, his choice of sport was again boxing and he used to spar frequently with a friend by the name of Barton. He also had enough interest in cricket to be a frequent spectator and, perhaps because of his size and strength, he trained with the Magdalen College rowing eight.

In the middle of it all, of course, Wilde was still Wilde, being celebrated and denigrated in fairly equal measure for the widely reported comment he made after decorating his room: 'I find it harder and harder every day to live up to my blue china.'

His oft-outrageous dress was also provocative, Wilde frequently sporting a huge coat and knickerbockers, together with hair worn very long for the time. Such dandyism predictably aroused the ire of many of his fellow students, and the memoirs of one of his fellows, recorded in Ellman's book, paints Wilde at his best.

According to Sir Frank Benson, Wilde was 'far from being a flashy aesthete', and few men 'had a ghost of a chance in a tussle with Wilde'.

By way of proof, Benson offers up an episode one evening where many of the young men of Magdalen had got together and decided on a plan of bursting into Wilde's room to give him a good pummelling and break up some of his furniture for a lark.

So it was that four of the heftiest of those most offended by his dandyism shouldered their way through Wilde's door while many others waited on the stairs to watch events unfold.

'The result was unexpected,' the biography recounts. 'Wilde booted out the first, doubled up the second with a punch, threw out the third through the air and taking hold of the fourth—a man as big as himself—carried him down to his rooms and buried him beneath his own furniture.'

The point of all this, Your Honour? None particularly, other than to note that if we can safely assume that good old Oscar didn't mind smacking people around a bit, then it might also be time to leave behind stories that recount in wonder that rugby players, footballers, boxers et al are anything other than a fairly Neanderthal breed.

And who knows whether Mike Tyson is not, even as we speak, penning an award-winning play in secret? We can only hope.

Sport and Sex

IT'S ABOUT SPORT and sexuality. And how renown in the former can often lead to greater activity in the latter . . .

Many moons ago, in a land far away, I was awakened at one am in my hotel room by a jostling hand on my shoulder.

'Fitz,' said my roomie and team mate (we were on a representative rugby tour at the time), 'I've got lucky. Do you mind doing some "one-eyed snoring", or do you want to hit the corridor?'

Translation: while tom-catting around the late-night bars and discos after the game, 'Tom' had found a partner willing for a one-night stand and I was being invited to either take a blanket and settle down in the corridor, or otherwise loudly feign sleep ('one-eyed snoring').

For him to ask me to vacate my room at that ungodly hour, for such a purpose, was well within tour etiquette—I would have asked exactly the same of him in the same circumstances—but for once the choice was relatively easy. Whereas usually I'd have taken my pillow and blanket and staggered off into the night, this night seemed transported direct from the North Pole and that option was out.

So, after obliging with some particularly loud snoring *twice* in the next fifteen minutes (my room-mate was a very young man), an odd thing happened. From the next bed, Tom simply got up and left. Never to return. Fifteen minutes later the phone rang.

'Fitz, it's me. Is she still there?'

'Yes . . .'

'Can you tell her I've had to go out urgently or something, and I'll see you in the morning. You understand.'

(Click.)

Translation: It was still only two am, the discos had not yet closed and he was going to try his luck *again*. Outrageous, and well out of bounds of tour etiquette, but that was just the way Tom was.

With no further use for feigning sleep, the girl and I got talking. Her name was Sheri, she was eighteen, and she was a hairdresser. She'd met Tom at about midnight, immediately recognised his name, if not his actual physiognomy, and it had gone from there. The truly extraordinary thing was she didn't seem at all upset by Tom's abandonment. She'd been with famous guys before, she confided, and you had to expect them to behave a bit weirdly.

Indeed. But what an odd kink it is in the cosmos which deems that famous names alone can be so sexually attractive. It's no secret that sportsmen particularly—so often away from home—soon realise the existence of this quirk, and sometimes take advantage of it. Most interesting of all though is when *other* people realise it and play the same card. Even when they're not sportsmen . . .

Take for example the case of a fellow by the name of Kevin Winn who was arrested in the United States last year and recently profiled in *GQ* magazine. Winn, the magazine said, 'has thinning hair, a pudgy baby face and a short, husky body'. In short, he looked nothing like your usual professional athlete.

But it didn't matter. Merely by using the *name* of a number of these athletes, and peppering his conversation with a line of knowledgeable sports patter, Winn managed to sleep with over a hundred women over three years—as well as frequently cleaning them out of a lot of money. His usual *modus operandi* when he walked into a bar on the east coast of the United States was to home in on an obviously gregarious bar-fly, introduce himself as the particular athlete, and then get the bar-fly to do the introducing from there. 'It gave me instant credibility,' he recounted.

From there he'd use his instant celebrity in the bar to work his way into a target woman's bed and purse.

Apparently it was amazingly easy. His famous name would give him instant access to everything, and it would all fall into place from there. He would usually claim that his bags had been lost in transit by the airline and one bag unfortunately had his wallet in it. Could they tide him over with some money meantime . . .

How could Winn survive pretending to be a famous athlete, when, by definition, there should be many people who knew what that athlete looked like?

Simply by not being too ambitious—he would usually only pick journeymen professionals to impersonate or otherwise athletes like hockey goalies or baseball catchers who, while famous, usually had their faces hidden behind masks.'

And besides, 'one of the keys to Winn's success was that he usually operated in that stratum of society where *USA Today* is the standard reference work and express checkout is the main social amenity'.

Winn knew other tricks to keep his credibility going after the initial contact. With one woman by the name of Michelle, Winn pretended to be Kevin Deneen of the Hartford Whalers and enjoyed the charade so much he decided to have something of 'an ongoing relationship'.

'He was so believable,' Michelle says. 'He'd call and say "I'm on my car phone", and it sounded like he was.' (Winn's trick was to pull rest-stop pay phones into his car and leave the motor running and the radio on.) 'He'd call and tell me he was in the locker-room after a game, and it sounded like that. He must have been in his bathroom or something.'

Or something.

Finally, though, the comeuppance. Winn was arrested for

impersonating Scott Bradley, a baseball catcher for the Seattle Mariners, and, in the process, doing yet another woman out of her chastity and money.

The woman was apparently convinced that Winn really was Scott Bradley right up until the moment she and Winn 'were in her Brighton bedroom, still sweaty from sex, and her mother called to tell her that Scott Bradley was on television'.

Sprung. Two eighteen-month sentences served concurrently were the final sentence. He should be out some time soon.

As for Tom, he's still going strong. Damn his eyes.

The Package Tour Profiteers
Reach A Tawdry Summit

THE NEWS CAME over the wire services just recently. In one day, thirty-two people—count 'em, *thirty-two* people—stood on the summit of Mount Everest. In one day.

Beneficiaries of the fact that there are now ice steps cut into the higher reaches of the mountain, together with fixed ropes and mountaineering companies who, for the price of $50,000, will do everything in their commercial power to get you up there on the roof of the world, one wonders if those thirty-two felt their achievement was just a fraction hollow, compared with what the first conquerors of the mountain felt four decades ago.

'My solar plexus was tight with fear as I ploughed on,' wrote Sir Edmund Hillary.

'I could look down 10,000 ft between my legs, and I have never felt more insecure. Anxiously, I waved Tensing (Norgay) up to me . . .

' "What do you think of it, Tensing?" And the immediate response: "Very bad, very dangerous!" "Do you think we should go on?" And there came the familiar reply that never helped you much but never let you down. "Just as you wish!" I waved him on to take a turn at leading.'

Sir Edmund is now seventy-two and lives in Auckland, New Zealand. Looking back this week on his historic climb, he recounted over the phone: 'Really, the thing was we had no idea of whether or not we were going to make it, whether we would ever be coming back down the same way. We were, of course, conscious that we were climbing where no-one had ever been.

'There was no certainty . . . we knew nothing of what lay before us, or even if it was possible to get to the top.'

After climbing what Hillary describes as 'a maddening series of bumps', they then came to what they realised was 'the last bump'.

This last bump, the summit itself, is apparently a rounded knoll of snow and ice, on which several people could stand at once. As to who actually stood on the summit first, Sir Edmund is initially cagey. 'We always used to tell people that we climbed it together, arm in arm, for in the end it did not really matter.'

Of course it doesn't matter, but really, who was the actual first? 'It makes no difference at all, but when we got to the summit I was just a few paces ahead of Tensing,' Sir Edmund says reluctantly.

On one side, a sheer precipice falling out to Tibet; on the other, a fractionally less daunting decline into Nepal.

Photo time.

'Tensing had been waiting patiently, but now, at my request, he unfurled the flags, wrapping them around his ice axe and, standing on the summit, held them above his head.

'Clad in all his bulky equipment and the flags flapping furiously in the wind, he made a dramatic picture, and the thought drifted through my mind that this photograph should be a good one, if it came out at all.

'I didn't worry about getting Tensing to take a photograph of me—as far as I knew he had never taken a photograph before and the summit of Everest was hardly the place to show him how.'

Indeed.

Tensing died in 1986, but Sir Edmund recounts: 'Even though we didn't know each other particularly well at the time we climbed Everest—his English wasn't very good—we managed to spend a lot of time together in later years and formed a great affection.'

Tensing Norgay ran a Himalayan mountaineering institute in his middle years, while Sir Edmund was the New Zealand High Commissioner to India.

These days Sir Edmund spends a great deal of time raising money for charitable institutions, particularly in the Indian sub-continent, and still travels widely. So it happened that when the thirty-two aforementioned climbers did reach the summit in a single day, Sir Edmund was in the area at the time.

'I was absolutely appalled,' he says.

'Mountaineering seems now to have become so very commercialised and it doesn't appeal to me at all. In my day it was the personal, individual challenge that was so exciting about it all. I have the feeling that these days a lot of people are doing it so they will have something to boast about to their friends.'

The way Sir Edmund speaks about it, one somehow gains the impression that ego had very little to do with his own ascent in June 1953.

'It just turned out that we were the first to climb it. My overwhelming sensation when on the summit of Everest was surprise, really. Surprise that somehow we were the ones that were first.'

While in this interview Sir Edmund does not recount what Tensing Norgay's words were at the time, an earlier account gives a good impression of what the Sherpa's feelings must have been.

'I turned and looked at Tensing. Even beneath his oxygen mask and the icicles hanging from his hair, I could see his infectious grin of sheer delight. I held out my hand and in silence we shook in good Anglo-Saxon fashion.

'But this was not enough for Tensing, and impulsively he threw his arm around my shoulders and we thumped each other on the back in mutual congratulations.'

My point? That this account seems so magnificent, whereas the modern way of paying your money and following the beaten path strikes one as so tawdry by comparison.

Avoiding l'Esprit de l'Escalier

THE FRENCH HAVE a name for it—*l'esprit de l'escalier*. The 'spirit of the staircase' is that feeling that comes upon you after you've had a raging argument with someone for half an hour, to and fro, neither one gaining the upper hand, when finally you've had enough. You stand up from the table, stomp to the door, slam it! and then loudly bang your way up the stairs . . . when suddenly it hits you.

That precise thing which you should have said to leave your opponent dead in the water . . . but it is too late to storm back down the stairs, unslam the door, retake your place at the table and unload it on them. You just have to wear the fact that you were too slow and the right moment for the perfect rejoinder—be it angry, romantic, profound or whatever—has gone. And all our lives are full of such moments, *n'est-ce pas*?

Actually, not quite all. History is at least lightly sprinkled with examples of people saying exactly the right thing at the right time, and has shown a marked propensity to record such moments for posterity.

Perhaps the most famous example is Sir Winston Churchill's reply to an infuriated Lady Astor's expostulation: 'Winston, if you were my husband I should put arsenic in your coffee!'

'Nancy, if you were my wife, I should drink it.'

Rarely has a *touché* been such a through-the-heart rapier, but for what it's worth, here are a few more instant retorts that have entered history for their sheer timeliness and rightness.

Perhaps the best are distinguished by a certain rich pathos. My own favourite comes from the recent political arena, in the televised American vice-presidential debates in 1988 between Dan Quayle and Michael Dukakis's running mate, Lloyd Bentsen.

The debate had been going for perhaps half an hour, with Quayle more and more eager to wrap himself in the robes of the great John F. Kennedy—another very young Senator who had proved that he could go on to make good—when Bentsen had had enough.

Quayle: '. . . just like President Kennedy . . .'

Bentsen: 'Senator, I knew Jack Kennedy. Jack Kennedy was a friend of mine. Senator, you are no Jack Kennedy.'

The video shows it still, Quayle pausing, stunned—a rabbit who has just been publicly wiped out but is still clinging to the bullbar—before rather lamely replying, 'That was a cheap shot, Senator.'

Cheap? *Cheap*? It was brilliant and arguably the best-aimed clod of earth to hit Quayle's coffin in the constant rain of clods that would fall on it over the next four years.

Also in the political arena, though from a couple of centuries earlier, comes this famous and timeless exchange between Lord Sandwich and John Wilkes.

Lord Sandwich: 'Really, Mr Wilkes, I don't know whether you'll die on the gallows or of the pox.'

John Wilkes: 'That depends, m'lud, on whether I embrace your principles or your mistress.'

Closer to home, a personal favourite comes from our own Prime Minister Billy Hughes. Prime Minister Hughes went with a friend to view his official prime ministerial portrait that was to hang in the national parliament. Hughes was a famously wizened fellow, not likely to be approached to tread the catwalk in his spare time, and a little nervous when first approaching the painting. But his friend was rather more gracious.

'I think it does you justice,' said he.

'It's not justice I want,' breathed a wistful Hughes in reply, 'it's *mercy*.'

It is in the realm of giant egos clashing, though, that some of the best rejoinders arise, and where is one to find bigger egos than Hollywood?

Best and brightest is perhaps the one from Margot Fonteyn, who was becoming increasingly irritated with Jean Harlow and her constant insistence on pronouncing the 't' in Margot . . . 'MargoT this, and MargoT that'. Finally, Fonteyn could stand it no more.

'No, Jean,' Fonteyn drawled, 'the "t" is silent, like the silent "t" in Harlow.'

From roughly the same era comes the time when Vivien Leigh was getting off the aeroplane on her first trip to Australia, only to be confronted by a reporter who had raced across the tarmac to blurt out 'Miss Leigh, Miss Leigh, what do you think of Australia?'

'I don't know,' the filmstar replied, 'You're standing in the way.'

Then there is the late, great Mae West, who upon meeting a young man who rather took her fancy, was nothing if not forthright.

Mae West: 'How tall are you, son?'

Young Man: 'Ma'am, I'm six feet and seven inches.'

Mae West: 'Let's forget the six feet and talk about the seven inches.'

Still in the theatrical field, Noel Coward was once told of the suicide of an actor he knew, a man whom he'd regarded as being not very bright. On asking how the man had killed himself, Coward was told that 'he shot his brains out'.

Coward's retort was as dry as it was swift: 'He must have been a marvellous shot!'

Rare is the witticism recorded from someone who is not

famous, but sometimes their mere propinquity to important historical players can give their words memorable weight.

History does not record the name of the attendant who woke Louis XVI in the wee hours at his Versailles palace in 1789 with the news that the Bastille had been stormed, but it has at least carefully noted this telling snatch of dialogue.'

Louis XVI: *'C'est un revolt?'*

Attendant: *'Non, sire, c'est un revolution.'*

While the written retort does not strictly qualify for this collection, some are simply too good to leave out.

George Bernard Shaw immediately comes to mind, in his reply to a society hostess who had sent him a formal invitation: 'Lady Grosvenor will be at home Thursday between four and six.'

Shaw's reply: 'Mr Bernard Shaw likewise.'

Then there is the English writer, Elinor Glyn, who sent off her book to a prospective publisher and included this rather haughty note: 'Would you please publish the enclosed manuscript or return it without delay, as I have other irons in the fire.'

By the next post, Glyn received the manuscript with the publisher's reply: 'Put this with your other irons.'

One of the rarest genre of such exchanges is perhaps the 'double-shuffle' or 're-retort', where a witty retort is unexpectedly topped by an even better reply. George Bernard Shaw once sent a telegram to the actress Cornelia Otis Skinner, who had opened in his *Candida* on Broadway (1935).

Shaw: 'Excellent! Greatest!'

Cornelia Otis Skinner replied: 'A million thanks, but undeserving such praise.'

Shaw: 'I meant the play.'

Skinner: 'So did I.'

But now to the rarest kind of exchange of all—the retort that is memorable not at all because of the wit, venom or pathos of the words, but reply through the circumstance of its utterance.

There is none better than the example of General Sedgewick, whose reply to a junior at the battle of Spotsylvania in the American Civil War earned him immortality. As the good general pranced up and down behind his rebel soldiers, exhorting them to ever greater efforts, one of his aides ventured to say: 'Sir, don't you think it would be a good idea if you were to present a less obvious target to those damn Yankees?'

'Don't be ridiculous!' boomed the fearless general. 'They couldn't hit an elephant at this dist----.'

At which point he tumbled off and died. No doubt apocryphal, but who cares? If that isn't what he actually said, that's what he *should* have said, if he was being at all fair dinkum.

From the battlefield to the literary field, and, of course, no-one looms larger than Oscar Wilde for quick comebacks. Most of these are too well known to repeat, but like the Beatles songs, it is not only the famous ones that are great . . .

Sir Lewis Morris: 'The press are neglecting my poems. It is a conspiracy of silence. What ought I do, Oscar?'

Oscar Wilde: 'Join it!'

Wilde himself, though, could also be the victim, as in this exchange with Sarah Bernhardt.

Oscar Wilde: 'Do you mind if I smoke?'

Sarah Bernhardt 'I don't care if you burn.'

Surely, surely, we assume that Oscar wishes he'd said that.

Lesser literary lights have also had their fair share of great retorts, though.

One Lord Young was at his best when confronted with a whingeing Alfred Austin, deploring the regrettably small amount of money that was available for poets.

'At least,' continued Austin, by way of cheering himself up, 'I manage to keep the wolf from the door.'

'How?' inquired Lord Young. 'By reading your poems to him?'

To America, and it was their great humourist of the 1930s, Robert Benchley, who, emerging drunk one afternoon after another session at the Round Table of the famous Algonquin restaurant, spied a man in uniform and commanded imperiously: 'Get me a cab!'

Man in uniform: 'Sir, I'll have you know I am an admiral in the United States Navy!'

Benchley: 'All right, then, get me a battleship!'

Legal circles, almost by definition, are characterised by constant verbal wrangling and it's only to be expected that over the last five centuries or so at least three or four clever things have been said.

Convicted criminal: 'As God is my judge I am innocent.'

Judge Norman Birkett: 'He isn't, I am, and you're not!'

Next we go to the following interchange, purportedly from a real Australian court, recorded in a book full of courtroom reminiscences entitled *Court in the Act*. This particular case involved a rape, where the victim alleged that she had only woken well after the accused had already penetrated her.

Prosecutor: 'When did you actually wake up?'

Witness: 'While he was raping me.'

Prosecutor: 'Do you mean he had just entered you?'

Witness: 'What do you mean?'

Prosecutor: 'Well could you estimate for us how far he had entered you before you woke up?'

Witness: 'Oh, yes, I'd say about that long.' (She indicates with her hands a distance of about 35 cm.)

His Honour: 'Well, Madam, I hope you won't drop off to sleep in the witness box, because I certainly could not wake you up.'

Similarly sexual in tone, though probably apocryphal, is the story of the wife claiming a divorce on the grounds of adultery who said she could prove it because her husband came home with 'a Venetian disease'. The judge asked what exactly 'a Venetian disease' was, whereupon her barrister stood up and said, 'Probably gondolier, your worship'.

No doubt.

Sport—and of all the many examples on offer there is surely none better than this exchange from the late seventies, between Joe Bugner and interviewer Hugh McIvanney. McIvanney had been implying that Bugner had been boxing 'doggo' against Ali, not trying to win, but just stay on his feet.

Bugner reacted angrily: 'Get me Jesus Christ, I'll fight him tomorrow!'

Hugh McIvanney: 'Joe, you're only saying that because you know Jesus has got bad hands.'

Ouch.

Keating

AUSTRALIAN PRIME MINISTER Paul Keating has just left for Britain to sit down with Her Majesty and talk to her about . . . about . . . about . . .

Well, just how *does* one broach the subject with Her Majesty that the general plan is to wipe her out as Australia's Head of State by the year 2000, haul down her image everywhere we see it, expunging every trace of her from our constitution, our statutes, our every place of official endeavour?

It seems hardly the proper thing to chat about over tea and scones at Balmoral Castle. For an event of such magnitude in the life of two nations, one would think the very least Keating could organise would be a Declaration of Independence and a medium-sized war to mark the occasion.

Yet the Prime Minister will make his statement of republican intent confident in the knowledge that he has the broad and growing support of his fellow citizens. The general feeling of the populace is that a republic is the coming thing sooner or later; Keating knows it, we know it, and the national suspicion is that the Queen knows it, too.

It is precisely this sense of inevitability which has robbed the republican debate of much of its real passion. At no time in the last eighteen months has the issue been as likely a topic of conversation at pubs and barbecues around the country as the likely teams in the football finals, as the latest details of Australia's humiliation of England in the crick . . . well, never mind.

More to the point, at no time has wider republican fervour reached heights that would result in the Australian equivalent of a Boston Tea Party. From the perspective of downtown Sydney, it looks less likely to be an earthquake or tornado that will usher in the new age than a gently rising tide which eventually engulfs all resistance.

In many ways it is a generational shift. While there is admittedly roughly one-third of the population who would prefer to retain the status quo, the rub is that from this group must be subtracted daily most of those names which appear in the obituary columns . . .

Our grandparents were all stauncher monarchists than our parents and we, in turn, are likely to be outshone in our anti-monarchal feelings only by our children.

Most of us from the younger generation can trace our republican leanings to the events of 11 November 1975, when our Governor-General, Sir John Kerr, dismissed our Prime Minister, Gough Whitlam, in the name of Her Majesty, Queen Elizabeth II.

Well, we never.

A famous political cartoon from soon afterwards shows a distressed Whitlam visible through a window of Buckingham Palace, as the Queen pokes her head out of the receiving room to ask a footman, 'What does "rough end of the pineapple" mean?'

In Australian parlance, receiving the 'rough end of the pineapple' means to have been given grossly unfair and high-handed treatment. And Whitlam was of course right in his estimation. Until that point, we had thought the monarchy was all just a matter of corgis and nice palaces, princes and princesses.

The upshot? Because the monarchial system was the purveyor of that rough end of the pineapple, it would have to go the same way Whitlam did. Tit for tat.

The media, of course, has played a significant part in the whole affair, most particularly since last year when Keating made his first public republic declaration, and the issue has played well in the papers and airwaves since. It has bubbled along as one of the stock issues—the story to turn to when there's not a lot else around, but one that is guaranteed to give lead bulletins and front-page stories proper *gravitas*.

The issue will play for many moons yet, in all likelihood until the drain of the obituary columns has left the republican forces weighty enough to reach a critical mass. That should happen somewhere around the turn of the century, just as Keating has planned.

It still begs the question of what *exactly* our Prime Minster will say to the Queen over high tea at Balmoral Castle. One version of their likely conversation has recently circulated around Australia, and it goes like this . . .

(With apologies to Her Majesty.)

'Your Majesty,' says Keating, 'Do you think you could make Australia a kingdom? That way I could be a king, and I'd really like that.'

'Well, no, Mr Keating, I really don't think that would be in order; I really don't think that could be done.'

'Well, then, Ma'am, umm. Do you think you could make Australia into a principality. That way I could be a prince, and that would be almost as good as a king.'

'No, no, really, I don't think I could do that.'

'Well, Ma'am, what could you do?'

'Well, Mr Keating, you know I could make Australia a country . . .'

President With an Energetic Way of Running Office

LISTEN UP. It's about how to go jogging—when you're the President of the United States. At least when you're President of the United States *and* on a brief visit to Sydney.

The easy part is getting a pair of sandshoes . . .

Then comes two police cars; three big black limousines; one intensive-care ambulance; some bomb-sniffer dogs commanded by the Australian Army; and twenty-five obviously armed men, speaking into walkie-talkies and looking very, very much like someone has just stolen their lunch—and they've got a pretty good idea who. Finally, get one black four-wheel-drive Chevrolet van bristling with antennae.

Around six-thirty am, on New Year's morn, you should roll over in bed and make a phone call to someone or other to the effect that you feel like going for a jog. From there, all the presidential machinery should move swiftly into place. Six armed men will immediately leave the hotel with the bomb-sniffer dogs to secure the way you want to jog. The convoy will then form up and an additional five police cars will charge ahead of you to clear the way.

(Incidentally, while you are doing this, never, ever worry about the expense of what you are doing. After all, you are the President of the United States, dammit. Most people travel with a spare tyre in the boot, while you, no kidding, travel with a spare Jumbo behind you in case Air Force One breaks down.)

When the convoy is formed up, you should get in Huge Black Limo Number Three. Number One Huge Black Limo should be loaded to the gills with men armed to the eyeballs, while the middle HBL should have a man in it who looks a lot like you, also in jogging gear. If anybody is going to launch a Howitzer shell at you, they're more than likely to mistake him for you, so you're still sweet as a nut.

Then get moving. The strange convoy, equipped to launch a nuclear war or withstand a commando attack, should go to a site about five minutes away from your hotel and one that can be totally secured from the outside—the Scots College, the exclusive boys' private school in Sydney's Bellevue Hill.

Totally ignoring all hitchhikers along the way, particularly any large Australian journalists who happen to have their thumb out, be sure to circle the school twice in your convoy until the word is passed from an unseen forward command post allowing Operation Jog to be executed. Glide smoothly into your destination, and then have the armed men scattter in all directions until you emerge triumphantly in full jogging regalia.

As you limber up, your armed guard men should frisk everybody within a hundred metres and put a metal detector all over them. One of those persons will be me—a reasonably law-abiding Australian citizen on Australian soil—but no worries. This is no time for technicalities. Your men should forcibly oblige him to 'assoom the position' and frisk him in the most incredibly personal places. You never know what sort of dangerous weapon might be secreted behind a scrotum.

Then, and only then, after checking that all his journalistic credentials are in full order should the men allow him to be ushered to the edge of the presidential orbit.

Speaking of which you, the President, should meantime have taken off on your jog of the oval. One secret service man five metres in front of you, one five metres behind you, and two right beside you—placed specifically in the most likely spot to stop an assassin's bullet.

Mr Bush runs well. I particularly liked the way he did not strain the heart whose every beat was to keep Dan Quayle from the presidency. On a roughly seven-minute-a-kilometre pace, the sixty-seven year-old completed six and a half laps of the large Scots oval in twenty minutes, twenty seconds.

He keeps up a sort of loping pace, periodically punctuated by a languid wave of the hand to the posse of photographers on the sideline. Apparently, he rarely jogs any more and sticks to an exercise-cycle in the White House basement. The reason he chose to jog here was that, while security may have been something of a nightmare to organise in relatively friendly Sydney, back home in Washington it is practically a logistical impossibility. So here he ran.

No sooner had he stopped than one of his minders handed him the presidential tracksuit top to prevent him from getting a chill, and he came over for a chat to the assembled forest of print and electronic media news-gathering devices.

He looks reassuringly fit, not breathing at all heavily. After covering weightier issues, in an incredibly convoluted manner of speaking in which there seemed no connection between the end of one sentence and the beginning of another, President Bush mentioned in passing that two of his New Year's resolutions were to do more fishing this year and also lower his time for two miles jogging so as to improve the fitness of his secret service men. Nice line, George.

And with that, the President departed. With a wave and the purring of limousine engines.

Operation Jog. Over and out.

Courageous Idol Knocked From the Pedestal

'I have wrassled with an alligator for this fight, I have tussled with a whale . . . handcuffed lightnin', put thunder in jail! Bad! Faaaast!'
Muhammad Ali

IT WAS TWO decades ago and it was arguably the greatest fight in the history of heavyweight boxing—called simply 'The Fight', in boxing parlance. Muhammad Ali versus George Foreman in Kinshasa, Zaire, November 1974, at four o'clock in the hot and humid African morning.

A masterful Ali, dancing thunder and lightning, against the young bull Foreman—simply the hardest hitter the world had seen since Babe Ruth.

'You heard about me for years, sucker . . .' Ali says to Foreman, eyeball to eyeball moments before the fight, '. . . all your life you been hearing about Muhammad Ali. Now, chump, you gotta face me!'

From the second round, Ali uses his previously unseen

rope-a-dope strategy. Covering up and leaning way back on the ropes he taunts Foreman: 'Is that the best you can do sucker?' 'Is that all you got chump?' 'You ain't got no punch! You in big trouble, boy!', while the frenzied Foreman empties many of his best shots all but uselessly into Ali's elbows and forearms.

Still, just at the end of the fourth, Foreman really does rock Ali with a crowbar blow, and for the first time replies to Ali: 'How's that?' he asks.

'Didn't hurt a bit!' replies the shaken Ali, and still later, pokes his tongue out at Foreman to show he is still in command.

The war continues: Foreman crashing on the door to get into Ali's skull; Ali pressing his whole body into the service of keeping it shut. Then, just before the eighth round, to Foreman's exhausted amazement, Ali stands on his stool in the corner and, using his hand as a baton, leads the delirious African crowd in a chant of '*Ali bomaye! Ali bomaye!*' (Ali kill him dead).

Which Ali does, just about.

With twenty seconds remaining in the eighth round, Foreman is so exhausted from battering on the door that he is now only pawing at Ali. For the first time his formidable defences are down. Ali, himself exhausted, still finds the energy to pounce.

To quote Norman Mailer's account of the fight: 'Then a big projectile, exactly the size of a fist in a glove, drove into the middle of Foreman's mind, the best punch of the startled night, the blow Ali had saved for a career . . . Foreman went over like a six foot, sixty-year-old butler who has just heard tragic news.'

Amid the wild seconds of euphoria after the bout, Ali briefly falls into a dead faint, before awaking to proclaim that he is, in fact, 'The Greatest'. Few were arguing at the time.

But odd how time has changed things so markedly. Foreman is now America's darling, with his own Pepsi commercial and everything, while Ali stands as the most tragic figure in sport, bar none.

Therein lies a tale . . .

The first sign came during the late seventies when, horror of all horrors, it became apparent that Ali was starting to slur his words, starting to shake visibly, to lose basic physical co-ordination. His condition deteriorated, and the most obvious diagnosis was 'punch-drunk'.

'Show me a great man and I will show you a tragedy,' Lord Byron once said, and this was surely the greatest tragedy possible for 'The Greatest'. That after years of dancing on the world stage, thunder and lightning in the ring, he should finish by barely shuffling around as a sad parody of what he once was.

But no. There *was* some hope after all.

In the early eighties we were told that it wasn't that he was punch-drunk at all, it was just that he had Parkinson's Disease, and there soon arose a doctor down in Mexico who claimed he could cure it using radical new methods, injecting a strange substance into his brain stems and so forth. Those of us who had always loved Ali for some reason we knew not quite why, followed with renewed interest as Ali went to Mexico.

But alas! Nothing came of it.

For the next seven years all was fairly quiet on the Ali front. He was sighted from time to time, always looking the worse for wear and on one notable occasion almost looking like a complete zombie, when in the ring before a Spinks-Tyson fight the dazed Ali raised a shaking hand of acknowledgment to the crowd.

But wait, more good news. Ali is neither punch-drunk nor does he have Parkinson's Disease, after all, we were told. He merely has a minor psychological problem arising out of being the world's most famous man, the one that most people wanted to touch and shake hands with.

After years upon years of people coming at him everywhere he went, he had subconsciously withdrawn into himself. But the same old Ali was still in there inside. Damn right he was. A little bit of psychological counselling, a little bit more retreat from the world to get himself together, and he'd be back, bigger 'n' better than ever, we were told by yet another doctor.

But still, nothing.

And now, the *very* latest. It has now been claimed that all of the preceding diagnoses have been false and what really ails him is pesticide poisoning.

I know, bizarre.

But one doctor believes it with great certitude, and as this is the man who has just been treating Ali at Hilton Head Hospital in South Carolina, he at least bears listening to.

'I don't think Ali is suffering from pesticide poisoning,' said Dr Rajku Medenica, over the telephone. 'I *know* he is.'

'That is what the tests clearly show.'

According to the doctor, Ali picked up the pesticide toxins in his system while going to his Pennsylvania training camp in the early seventies.

But to the point. Can Dr Medenica's treatment called *plasmacytopheresis*, or 'cleansing of the blood'—actually cure Ali?

'Not completely,' he says, 'but certainly, if he follows the course I have set him, and returns to me every month, I think we shall see much of the old Ali returning.'

The doctor reports that the rest of Ali's health is fine.

'His intellect is excellent,' he says, 'muscle strength is good, his kidneys good, cardiovascular is excellent.'

Terrific. But it's his brain that we want.

Ali has now undergone three three-hour treatments and Dr Medenica says they have been successful, but the full effect won't be apparent until the drug therapy has worn off.

Here's hoping. But judging from past experience . . .

It might be just that, like the Americans refusing to believe that such a lowdown loser as Lee Harvey Oswald could ever kill the great Camelot King, John F. Kennedy, and thus embrace any half-baked conspiracy theory that comes along, the rest of us are in a similar bind with Muhammad Ali. Tell us anything, but don't tell us that the great Muhammad Ali simply got hit on his head so often that he went punch-drunk. *Anything*, but not that.

What Superman really did need, it will in all likelihood turn out, was the good sense to hang up the gloves about seven years before he actually did. But I'd still *love* to believe it was pesticides.

Allan Langer

ANOTHER DAY, ANOTHER DOLLAR. And after finishing another hard day's work making carriages for Queensland Railways in their Ipswich workshop, Harry Langer would always return home to the weatherboard on Ferrett Street to much the same sound hurtling over the top of the house—the sound of his four sons playing football against each other out the back.

They grow backyards pretty big up Ipswich way, and the Langer backyard was a big 'un even by that city's standards. Plenty big enough for the boys to play full-on football and have a fight at the same time, and they rarely missed the opportunity. Usually, it was the same division: Allan, the youngest and smallest, would always be drawn to play with oldest son Cliff, against the middle two, Neville and Kevin.

Funny that Allan seemed to all but hold his own in these games even as a four-year-old, but then he'd always seemed a pretty tough kid even when judged against the toughness of his brothers.

'It was pretty full-on,' Allan says, 'but at least it kept us off the streets. We usually had either pretend Test matches or Brisbane club matches and we'd keep playing till it got dark. Then mum would only let us go to bed after we'd washed the grass stains off.'

Such football was to be a good grounding in the game for the man who would go on to be Broncos captain and Australian halfback, but there was an awful lot of football to be played and hard work to be done before he'd reach that exalted status. Sometimes, if ever the brothers would tire of beating each other, they would combine forces and play backyard football against the only other family in the area with enough brothers to give them a good game —the Walters family. There were five Walters boys—Brett, Steve, Andrew, and the twins, Kevin and Kerrod—and they played in a similar way to the Langers, which is to say full-on tackle.

'Yes mate, it was hard football, very hard,' Langer says. 'I certainly didn't take it easy on them.'

So who would win these backyard inter-family Test matches?

'I better say the Langers, mate, because my brothers and me really did give them a bit of a touch-up. Mostly we'd have to stop because Steve would always run away crying.'

If Langer learned a lot of his basic skills from such games, maybe too he learnt something about on-field leadership.

'He was always the boss,' recalls his mother, Rita, 'and I can remember him always yelling at his brothers all the time.'

'Always trying to get us to play the game *his* way,' adds brother Neville, 'and always belting me first because I was the next littlest to him in size.'

As well as backyard football, there was also school football and club football, and soon after that rep football. A bloke couldn't live by football alone though, at least not at fifteen, and his first job out of school was as a truckie's offsider with the Ipswich general store, Waltons, at the salary of $120 a week.

'I used to have to carry furniture and that, dryers, washing machines, and all that sort of stuff. Just moving it from one place to another,' he says. 'I used to find it pretty hard sometimes.'

True enough, says Trevor Wright, the truckie who it was Langer's job to help. Still living in Ipswich, and still driving the truck, Wright recalls Langer was willing to try to lift anything, no matter how big, and most often did.

'Mostly, you'd just see this washing machine moving along as if it was walking by itself,' Wright says. 'And you could see this mop of blond hair showing up just over the rim. He was a pretty good offsider and mostly always laughing, joking around, you know?'

There was one drawback though.

'He couldn't stop thinking about football. Always had his boots and his football gear in the cab and if ever we were passing his footie ground in the afternoon he'd just jump out. I'd yell out "hang on, you can't go yet, it's not 5 o'clock!" and he'd yell back over his shoulder something like "I'll work through lunch tomorrow!" and that would be it.'

During his time at Waltons, Langer began a relationship with the woman who would become his wife, Janine.

'We went to the same primary school and high school,' Langer says, 'And she never liked me at either. Then one day at Waltons, she just saw me lifting a fridge or something, I don't know, and maybe it was my muscles, but that was that and I took her out and we've been together since.'

Langer joined the council as a worker on the road gang for $200 a week.

'It would get that hot in the summer out on the roads,' he recounts, 'that you could hardly breathe it was so hot and gee, I used to get burnt.

'Always out on the road, always building the bloody roads, mixing the concrete, making the kerbs, all that sort of stuff. It wasn't easy trying to lift jack-hammers, crowbars and all that.

'For my footie, I never did weights but gee I lifted a lot of that sort of stuff.'

The hard physical labour wasn't the only hassle. As the youngest bloke on the road crew, it was also Langer's job to boil the billy.

'I used to have to get it ready by exactly 9.30 and if it wasn't ready by 9.30, the blokes weren't happy, I can tell you they weren't happy. And I hated it, specially when it was sometimes wet weather 'cos you couldn't get the bastard lit, the wood wouldn't light and they'd still want their billy boiled at 9.30 on the dot . . .'

But then, in mid-1987, something happened which would take him away from all that.

Even though he was playing in only an Ipswich club side, he was picked in the State of Origin side. Picked to play halfback inside 'The King', Wally Lewis, under coach Wayne Bennett, and against the cockroaches of the south.

Preceding his selection, there had been a heated debate in the Queensland league community as to whether or not Langer was good enough to take over from the injured Mark Murray.

The names of those against him were formidable. 'Wally didn't want me, Wayne didn't want me, a lot of the other players didn't want me,' Langer says.

But at least there was still one guy in his corner whose opinion counted for a lot: his coach at Ipswich, the one and only Tommy Raudonikis.

'The one guy who really stood up for me and said I should be picked in the side was Tommy. He told 'em to go and get stuffed in *Rugby League Week* and said that I was good enough. I really owe Tommy for that.'

Not that his troubles were over. When he turned up at Brisbane's Roma Street Travelodge to find he was rooming with Bobby Lindner, one of the Queensland forwards most vocal against his selection, there were no apologies.

Then, in one of the early team meetings, there was open discussion between Bennett and Lewis as to how best to go about covering for Langer's presumed defensive deficiencies.

'They were trying to see where they could hide me in the defensive line, in the second line or out wide, and I just had to sit there,' he says.

There was no Raudonikis on hand this time to speak for him and it would have been inappropriate for Langer to make an outburst, but help was at hand.

Having listened to the discussion for as long as he could, Paul Vautin stood up and interjected;

'Hey, he's a *Queenslander*! He won't let us down. He'll play where he normally plays.'

Which Langer did and acquitted himself well. The next year, as the incumbent Origin halfback, he returned to Brisbane full-time to play the with new-born Broncos and . . . his big-time rugby league career was truly launched.

The years passed, the way they do in those 1950s movies when the pages on the calendar turn over when a sudden gust of wind hits, and before Langer knew it, it was March 1994.

He was doing well. He was captain of the Broncos, Australian halfback, most popular person in Queensland, and rich. Between the money paid to him by the Broncos and the money he earned in many endorsements, he was able to provide a comfortable lifestyle for Janine and their two daughters.

And now, as always, there was another journalist who wanted to talk to him.

This one from Sydney, one of hundreds who had made the trek.

The journo was talking about something he'd seen on the box the other night where Langer had jinked left, then right, then . . . right again going through a gap the defence had not had time to even see, let alone try to close, and he was in under the posts for another try.

In response to the obvious question, like HOW DOES HE DO THAT?, Langer waxes a kind of matter-of-fact disinterest.

'I don't know. It's off the bat. It just happens,' he says.

'You don't go out and score tries, according to some plan, it just comes like that and you feel where you should go next.'

Part of Bennett's grand plan is to have someone as capable as Langer out on the field calling all the shots, and the coach himself has no hesitation in naming Langer as 'an absolutely fantastic captain, the best man I could hope to have out there, to keep the players' minds on the job, to get them "up".'

Not much of which happens in the dressing-room before the game.

Langer's account of what he usually says in the dressing-room is off-hand: 'I'll say a few things, that's all—you know, like, we've got to show a lot of commitment today and everyone's got to go out there and show 100 per cent and it will make everyone's job a lot easier.'

It is out on the field when things occasionally go astray that Langer's captaincy comes to the fore. Though again, it is in his own fashion. When put on the spot as to what he says to the players when standing behind the goal posts after a runaway try had been scored against them in the first two minutes, Langer is at something of a loss.

'I don't say much really . . . what do you say when something like that has happened? The players all know what's on, I don't need to tell 'em.'

When it's a question of what he does, he is on much surer ground.

'I'll try and get the forwards geed up again right away . . . make two or three tackles in a row on their big blokes or something . . . you know something like that usually gets 'em right back into it.'

Does he ever think, in quiet moments, what might have been his fate if his skill at football hadn't entirely transformed his life?

Yes he does, damn right he does. Thinks about it a hell of a lot in fact.

And what does he think he'd be doing?

'Mate, I think I'd probably still be on the council boiling that bloody billy,' he says. 'I'm just glad I had football on my side. I got a few lucky breaks and it's moved me along. One day I want to put a lot back into it.'

Kieren Perkins

THE CURIOUS THING about someone like Kieren
Perkins is that of the ten billion humans who ever lived, he's the
absolute best there ever was at one thing.

From the time when a few disgruntled travellers on
Noah's Ark decided to make a break for it and swim to a
nearby island, to at least last night when this book went to press,
no-one has ever swum 1,500m faster than he has.

At his fastest, Perkins covers 1,500m in, in, . . . hang on . . .
tell 'em Kieren: '14 minutes, 43.48 seconds.' That he knows the
figure so readily down to the last hundredth of a second is
normal for someone in his line of endeavour.

Breaking world records with gargantuan effort, then setting out to break them again is what he does with his time. It is
what has made him famous, will make him wealthy, and the
number, let's look at it again—14:43.48—is the star by which he
steers much of his life.

'To get down to 14 minutes 30 seconds—that is the goal,'
Perkins says.

'Breaking 15 minutes was the big thing, but we've done that and it's now time to move on to the next thing.'

Driving his sleek sports car with the smoothness of cream, Perkins is this morning making a trek from the Channel Ten studios nestled in the green hills above Brisbane (where he works one day a week as a TV sports reporter), down to the city proper.

In person, he is surprisingly slight in build and a tad taller than he seems in the water.

The oddest thing about him though is that despite spending something like six hours a day, six days a week, hovering just below the point of total exhaustion churning up and down a pool (what sort of nutter would choose that as a way of life anyway?), he has somehow emerged as an affable and interesting bloke.

'I know it looks weird to choose a lifestyle which to some looks like putting your head in a bucket of water half of the time,' he says with a laugh, 'but the thing is I really enjoy it.

'I liken it to driving—you're watching the road, you know what you're doing, but at the same time your mind will be turning over a hundred different things. That's another reason this Channel Ten job is so good for me—it means I'm out and about, meeting people, working, and not just losing myself entirely in swimming, which can be a problem for young swimmers particularly.'

That said, the training is still cripplingly constant and long. By 9 o'clock this morning he'd racked up 7km. This afternoon, he'll rack up another seven.

But to the point. Like, how on earth can he bleeding well do that, week-in, week-out, all month, all year, for ALL HIS FLAMING LIFE?

'I have days sure, where it's raining, I'm tired, and I wake up and I don't want to do it, and I say to myself, "no, no, no, I'm not getting up!",' he says.

'But when that happens I just go on auto-pilot, not thinking about it, just doing it.' And his auto-pilot, after all, has an extremely precise regimen to follow.

'The alarm goes off at 5.17 and I know I have to be up and out of bed at 5.22. That gives me two minutes to doze and three minutes to think about getting up but still enjoy being under the covers,' Perkins says.

'When I'm up, it takes me exactly 10 minutes to do my stuff, get dressed, have my drink, and be in the car ready to go by about 5.32, and then another 10 minutes to get to the pool.'

This schedule gets him to his pool at 5.43 am, a full two minutes before the gates open at 5.45, and it is this gap which provides what he claims are his best two minutes of the day. Sitting quietly in his car in the soft early morning light, he thinks about things.

'All sorts of things. I love those two minutes. It's just very quiet, very . . . reflective, and I think what I've got ahead of me. It's a settling thing.'

Then through the gates, towel down, 15 minutes of stretching, and into the pool and away. On and on and on and on and on.

Did he never wonder, in the quiet watch of the night, at the philosophical base of what he is doing, wonder what, at the end of the day, is the point of pushing himself like that to make a record that will inevitably be broken by someone else anyway?

'No. I don't think about it like that,' he says. 'Unfortunately, thought is one of the biggest problems with trying to be an athlete, because you end up thinking too much and come up with reasons not to do it.'

'The way I approach it is like that Nike ad—"Just do it!"— that's my favourite slogan, because it's the way you achieve your goals.'

Little of Perkins' singleminded, almost obsessional drive to achieve his goals appears to have come directly from his parents. Or at least they never pushed him anywhere he didn't want to go.

He only began swimming earnestly as a nine-year-old, after he ran through a plate-glass window in his home. The gashes over his body required 87 stitches, and time spent in the pool was deemed the best way to rehabilitate a particularly badly hurt leg.

'And I loved it and stayed with it,' he says.

'Mum and dad were happy that I'd found a sport I loved because they thought sport was good for a child, but they never pushed me to train hard.

'They never had high expectations of what I would achieve. They always said, "If you've done your best you can be happy" and it's never changed.

'I always wanted to do the best I could and I was lucky enough for my best to be *the* best.'

Brr. Brr. Brr. And that'll be your mobile phone, Kieren.

It's his father. Can he hand him over for a chat? Sure.

So is it true Mr Perkins that you and your wife never pushed Kieren?

'Absolutely true. In many ways we were dead set against it, and worried that he was pushing himself too hard. In fact we still worry that he pushes himself too hard.'

Fair enough.

The sports car momentarily stops beside road workmen doing some heavy leaning on their shovels. One of them though, suddenly catches sight of Perkins and digs his mate in the ribs, nodding in our direction. The gesture is soon repeated down the line, until by the time Perkins nudges the accelerator and we start purring forward, all 15 of them are standing as a kind of solemn, silent sentinel, shovels in hand, standing up straight, watching us pass.

Perkins appears oblivious to it all—as if he has long ago ceased to notice that people notice him—and lets the 150 or so horses under the bonnet have their head.

Motoring now, hugging the corners and accelerating out of them on this beautiful Brissy day. So how does he feel about being famous? Does he like it?

'Yes and no,' he says.

' "Yes" to everything, except for the 'no' part and that is the constant attention which can be wearing.

'Although I would like some anonymity, I know I won't get it. And I know because of who I am and what I do, I shouldn't really expect it either. It comes with the territory.'

What also comes with that territory, at least, is the potential to earn a lot of money through sponsorship, endorsements, and so forth.

Perkins makes no apology for the money he earns in this way.

'I want to go on for another seven years and that means a long time where I'll be concentrating on swimming and not on career, so it's important to me that I achieve a certain financial security from what I'm doing now.'

Luckily, sponsors are falling from the skies for him, sprouting in his garden, popping up through bathroom drains and slipping under the door.

'It's going well,' he says.

'There was a time there where—because I was getting older, getting stronger, getting smarter and more experienced in racing—my times would automatically get better every time I got in the pool to race and I would expect that.

'Now I've come to the realisation that I can't just go faster every time I get in the pool, it's just impossible.'

Instead, what he plans to do is choose his moments and . . . And hold it. Unfortunately, I've got to get out at the next stop.

All up, what has he learnt about this race that he has devoted so much of his life to being the best in?

'What I've learnt is that the 1500 is all about relaxation and rhythm. Picking up a rhythm and keeping your stroke in line and in tune. Making immediate adjustments to your stroke if ever it falters.

'That's one of those things that I hope will improve for me as I get older—to be able to stay better with the perfect rhythm and be able to correct it more quickly if I stray.'

And there's my destination now. Thanks for the lift. You seem a particularly happy man Kieren . . .?

'I am a very happy man' he replies simply.

'I enjoy it all. I'm living life to the fullest, and I'm probably one of the few people who can say I do what I love for a living and I love what I do.'

Greg Norman

HE'S BACK. Australia's most famous sportsman, the man we love to hate, but sort of love, anyway. Greg Norman has returned to the land of his forefathers, the land where those big bronzed shoulders first sent the ball soaring off to the far green horizons, the land where . . . you get the picture.

Norman is taking part this very day in a tournament titled, appropriately enough, the Greg Norman Classic.

Sigh, like Disraeli growling, 'When I want to read a good book, I'll write one,' Norman is now big enough to create his own tournament whenever he's of a mind to play one. Sigh.

If all nations may be regarded as having a 'relationship' with their most famous sports heroes, then Australia's relationship with Greg Norman has been rather troubled. We admire him, of course, for charging down the international fairways year after year, looking like a million dollars and annually earning fifteen times that amount in the process. We are a tad in awe of him for coming back to win the British Open Championship for the second time—just when everybody said he'd never recover from the psychological scarring caused by Bob Tway's and Larry Mize's outrageous chip shots at the US PGA and Masters Tournaments respectively—to win at the death in 1986.

Sure we love all that. But to the list of our annoyances . . . (*How long have you got?*)

We are annoyed, to begin with, at the manner of his latest arrival in Australia. The rest of us losers have to arrive by regular airlines, then line up for an hour to go through the passport authority, before elbowing our way through the luggage forest. Norman arrives, get this, by his own private jet worth fifteen million dollars—a Gulfstream Aerospace III, whatever that is—and is whisked to his luxury hotel by limo, before we've even got time to stagger to the end of the taxi queue. Not that there's any crime in being rich, of course, it's just that being so publicly rich gets up our collective nose a bit.

We are annoyed that when interviewed, Norman frequently talks like a half-baked American about all the 'opport-ooo-nities' available to him. Backward barbarians that we are, we like to pronounce it 'opport-u-nities'.

It's one thing to be one of us made good, and quite another to have made so good that the feeling grows that he doesn't see us any more, so much as look down the end of his nose at us. We are annoyed by a lot of his public utterances. While it's OK for *us* to say that he's a champion player, we start to lose the plot a little when he says, as he did recently, that 'I was in awe of myself out there today'.

Same thing with his nickname. It's fine for *us* to call him 'The Great White Shark', because that seems an appropriate enough moniker for one so talented and all-round gleaming white, but when we hear that his secretary answers the phone at his Florida headquarters with 'Hello, Great White Shark Enterprises . . .' and that there is now an entire line of golfing paraphernalia available with 'Great White Shark' all over it, one is less inclined to be quite so openly admiring.

This mild antipathy is not, as a general rule, one shared by the professional golf writers. At his press conference in Sydney yesterday, the feeling in the air from these hardened golf journalists was still solid awe—awe at proximity to one so great.

Part of Norman's charm to these people is encapsulated in a book recently released in Australia about Norman, which quotes Jim Murray of the *Los Angeles Times*.

'Best of all,' Murray wrote, 'he looks like what you think a world-class athlete should look like. The way you'd look if you made your living in sports. If you think this common, you don't know golf. They got guys in this game who can't see without glasses. They get some who can't see too well *with* glasses.

'Not our Greg. Greg Norman looks as if he was made by Michelangelo . . . he doesn't try to hit it, he tries to *disintegrate* it. He slides into the ball at impact like a cop crashing into a locked door in a vice raid.'

Soon, he'll be gone again. Off to the northern skies in his jet, to play a few more million-dollar tournaments, perhaps stage a few more of his own Classics and oversee the construction of the 'dozen golf courses I currently have under construction in Asia'.

Sigh. What's on the telly?

Dennis Lillee

DENNIS LILLEE ON THE BLOWER, calling from somewhere in Perth from his car phone, with a basic question.

'Why, mate?'

Like, why would anyone want to do another interview with him, was there anything left to say? Surely the story has been done to death?

Yes, well Mr Lillee, without being too mealy-mouthed about it, perhaps because you're pretty much the most famous Australian sportsman of your generation, and seeing as I'm going to be in Perth anyway for the end-of-season cricket dinner, it seems the obvious thing to look you up.

'Oh. Well perhaps we could . . . hold on . . . I've just seen this dickhead who I don't want to see me. Just a sec while I duck down . . .' 'It's OK, he's gone. Now, all right, let's see how we go, let's have a chat at the din . . . hang on, he's back, pain that he is . . . No, it's all right, he's gone . . . All right. Let's just have a chat at the dinner and see how we go.'

Sure enough, a slap on the back reveals Lillee standing

behind me, resplendent in his black tie and hand out-stretched as he helps himself to a seat at the table.

Surely it must be like this for Lillee with just about every adult Australian he meets for the first time. He's mouthing the usual 'gidday-how'd-ya-be?'s', while his interlocutor is on momentary auto-pilot—'yeh, bewdy, how're you?'—all the while trying to make a connection between the hundred memories they have of the cricketer, with the man before them. For myself, for what it's worth, visions come of standing on the Hill as a ten year old, shyly joining in the chant of 'Lilleeee . . . Lilleeee . . . Lilleeee' as the man charged in. And in the long hot summer of 1975-76, my father's head continually popping up from somewhere in the tomato patch, holding the tranny and yelling to us kids the great news: 'Lillee's got another one!'

Yes, he looks good, does Lillee. Of course, he's older, a tad heavier, a lot balder. But then aren't we all? Within those parameters he looks very fit and friendly. Not only does he not mind a bit covering for you until your faraway look has gone, but he even helps you pick up the pieces of the conversation as if he's barely noticed a thing.

So what's he up to these days?

Plenty. Plenty, An awful lot . . . just a sec . . . we have been interrupted by a silver-haired lawyerly-looking type who has timidly approached our table for a genuine Lillee autograph. No problem at all, Dennis signs with the instant flourish of one who has done the same thing tens of thousands of times before and seems to do it almost without thinking, though his innate friendliness to the bloke seems genuine enough.

'Where were we?' he asks.

What you're up to these days. Lillee is just about to respond when an old teammate comes up, all hail-fellow-well-met and roaring laughter and it's another few minutes before the former fast-bowler can extricate himself.

Another quick autograph for a middle-aged woman, a couple more handshakes and back-slaps in passing, a big 'hello' from a passing waitress, and finally Lillee gets it out.

He's been busy, yes, very busy. He's living with his wife

and two children in Perth, but sometimes gets so busy he spends a lot more time away from them than he'd like. Specifically, he runs a few cricket coaching clinics, is associated with the running of a Perth nursing home, plays the stock market, has a couple of small building developments he's getting up, has been doing some media work and most lately, he's been busy in this new business venture.

It's a venture, as it turns out, which seems made for him as it relies heavily on a level of sporting fame that few other than Lillee can bring to bear.

'Mate it's called Field of Dreams,' he announces, not without pride, and spins the tale from there.

The basics of the concept are selling signed sporting memorabilia in outlets throughout Australia. Boxing gloves signed by Muhammad Ali, baseball bats with the Micky Mantle moniker upon them, cricket balls with the signature of D.K. Lillee right there—that you, too, can hold and touch and have under your own hand, all for a lousy $80 or so. All replete with a guarantee of authenticity, which states the sports star both signed *and* handled the particular merchandise.

After a bit of a false start last year, Lillee and his associates hope to get the whole thing properly up and running in the next few months, with about 40 outlets around Australia.

They've already opened a few shops, with AFL footballer Gary Ablett, Allan Border and Lillee proving the three biggest home-grown sellers of sporting memorabilia.

Hmmmm. Does he not think it a very strange thing that there is a whole market out there for things that are made instantly more valuable simply by putting his signature on it?

Well, a bit odd perhaps, but that was neither here nor there for him. The fact is there's a market for it, it makes a lot of people happy and who is he to argue?

In pure business terms, it's not a bad deal. Lillee has, after all, an all-but-unlimited supply of signatures in him, and he'd also have to be close on being the Australian expert when it comes to the power of fame.

He first got a real idea of how weird it all was when with the Australian team on the Ashes tour of 1972. Mick Jagger himself, Jumpin' Jack Flash in the flesh, had come down to watch the game and inevitably gravitated to the dressing-rooms at the end of the day.

'You couldn't believe it,' recounts Lillee. 'What he was like in our dressing-room. I mean this was Jagger probably at the height of his fame, and we were pretty amazed to be around him, but he was incredibly shy around us. He just loved the cricket . . . said he "thought it was like ballet".' And so it went. Lillee and Jagger ended up as best buddies, with Jagger making a point of spending a lot of time with Lillee in the West Indies when the Stones and the Australians happened to be touring there at the same time at the end of the 1970s.

'Great guy,' says Lillee. '*Terrific* guy.'

Oddly enough, Jagger reminds him a bit of Jack Nicholson, another guy he gets on well with. And of course there were many such enormous celebrities that the West Australian palled around with over the years.

The only one to really knock back any friendliness on his part was the Queen, who once declined to give him an autograph.

But what the hey? All up, it hasn't been a bad sort of knock-about-the-world life for a man whose proud claim is that 'my mother was a shop-assistant and my father was a truck driver'.

If Lillee is comfortable with his own fame, understands its nature, and is prepared to dole out infinitesimally small parts of it as part of a business, he nevertheless seems entirely unimpressed with it on his own account.

'Mate, most of it is just a lot of crap,' he said. 'Most of that over-the-top stuff that was written about me. I mean what is there really to say? I'll tell you what would do me: "He was a good bowler who got stuck in and had a go." '

'I wouldn't say I was any bowling genius, or was born with any fantastic talent, but I had a go and did my best. That's all there is to say really.'

He seems genuine in such off-hand dismissal of his own celebrity.

When asked in passing, for example, as to exactly how many Tests he has played, he is not sure. 'Either 69 or 70 Tests, you'll have to look it up,' he said. And although he thinks he 'took about 355 wickets', again it quite genuinely doesn't seem to be a number that pops immediately into his mind.

Lillee returns to his table as the night is swept away with many dignitaries and one interloper going to the podium—everyone making mention of Lillee's august presence among them. At each glowing mention of his name, Lillee neither shifts uncomfortably in his seat nor smiles nor nods. Such reverential treatment seems to be neither here nor there for him—it's just there, the way it has been for the past twenty years or so.

By midnight the crowd is starting to thin, except for a cluster around the middle of the room. Sure enough, that is Lillee's table. Just a few more people wanting a bit of a chat, a bit of a slap on the back, maybe just a small autograph.

Catching my eye, Lillee winks and gives a cheerio wave as he signs someone's program, before helping himself to some more wine. Without anything you can put your finger on, he gives the impression of one for whom the night is still very, very young.

The short answer of what Lillee is up to these days? He's enjoying himself. Hugely.

Andrew Gaze

AUSTRALIAN BASKETBALLERS CALL IT 'The Show'. It is their name for the centre of the basketballing universe, the place they all aspire to get to in the wildest of all their wild dreams, the American National Basketball Association competition.

Made famous by such luminaries as Wilt Chamberlin, Michael Jordan, Larry Bird and Magic Johnson, the NBA is, to Australian basketballing eyes, a fast, rich and gloriously glamorous place. A place where the huge stadiums are always sold out, where there are so many television cameras they can look up your left nostril if they want to, and the average salaries are twenty times as high as in Australia. Yet, while all Australian professional basketballers aspire to play in the Show, those who actually get the call are fewer even than 'precious few'. Australian basketball captain Andrew Gaze is now the other one.

After many and many a moon of waiting, of quietly despairing that perhaps he was destined to miss out after all, the twenty-eight year old at last got the call at his home in Melbourne last month. The guy on the other end of the line, from the Washington Bullets, quickly came to the point:

The team was having a bad run of injuries and was wondering if he would like to come to the States, initially for a ten-day contract, and . . . and . . . hello . . .? hello . . .?

Gaze was already on his way to Tullamarine.

The two ten-day contracts he served with the Bullets comprised nine games where he averaged four points a game and ten minutes of court time. Mere numbers, though, do nothing to reflect his deep satisfaction.

'I suppose in terms of an entire career in basketball, it might look to some like a very small blip, but for me it was the ultimate, the thing I'd dreamed of doing most of my life and there's nothing that really comes close to it,' Gaze says.

Right from the first moment, things were a little different from what he was used to: the basketball itself was more aggressive, faster, more exotic in its movements and just generally . . . 'bigger than 'Big-Time'.

His fellow players, for example. Millionaires, every damn one of them. With a salary cap of $US17 million ($24 million) among twelve players, this was not surprising, and although Gaze's own monetary reward was a paltry $US1000 a day, there were no hard feelings.

'I think they just paid me out of petty cash from the secretary,' he says with a laugh.

Were his millionaire team-mates at least welcoming to him, the poor relation?

'Absolutely. I was amazed and very heartened by it, the whole organisation seemed to accept me very easily,' he says.

On this subject, though, Gaze got a word of warning from fellow Australian Luc Longley, now playing with the Chicago Bulls.

'Luc called me up and I was telling him how terrific everyone was being, when he said, "Yeah, but be careful . . . everyone's your mate until, one: you start cutting into their court time, two: you start making more money than they do, or three: the coaches start favouring you".'

As it turned out, Gaze wasn't there long enough for any of

the above to take place.

More important was his interaction with the opposition. From his first game, against the Denver Nuggets at home, they were coming at him. Moving quicker than he was used to, jumping higher to block his shots, causing a sometimes-blinding blur of defensive movement between him and the basket. And one other thing:

'They were always "talking trash" to me . . .'

Come again?

'You know . . . talking trash.'

Talking trash is apparently the American basketball version of sledging—a fairly constant diatribe of insults that one is subject to throughout the game by one's immediate opponent. And as the new boy on the block, our Andrew got at least his fair share and then some . . .

Suddenly, Denver were flicking the ball around the key looking for the best opening. For Gaze, the crowd noise seemed suddenly blotted out as he became conscious only of his own throbbing adrenalin and the urgent need to scramble to cover his man, when this very same fellow started in:

'Oh God, I got a slow white boy on me, a rookie, *God*, he's soooo *slow*! Gimme the ball, man! Gimme the ball! I gonna dunk it down on this white boy's heeaaaad!'

Same thing when moments later Gaze had possession of the ball and was helping to mount the Washington attack. Another Denver player opened up: 'Are you kiddin' me, mannnn? Are you *kiddin*' me? You cain't play this game! You cain't get past me! I'm gonna take this ball off you and stuff it up your aaaaaassss!'

So what did our man do in response to such provocation? Did he give him a taste of Australian elbow/fist/forearm? Did he at least tell him: 'Yeah, well, your motherrrr wears *big* army boots!'?

None of the above.

'I just played,' Gaze said. 'That sort of stuff is not a big deal, even in Australia, and I just entirely ignored it. I'm afraid I've never been able to talk and play basketball at the same time.'

Gaze ended up acquitting himself well in his debut, and

earned the public praise of his coach in the press the next day, with the team having scored a rare win in what had been a long line of defeats.

In the dressing room, the new chum was surprised by what seemed little joy or back-slapping—just as he had been surprised before the game began that there had been little emotional build-up.

'Basically, there are so many games over there, eighty-four in just five months of the competition, that neither the team nor the crowd can get themselves "up" for every game,' Gaze said.

'There's just no way you can do it, because there's only so much adrenalin to go around. The difference between a winning locker-room and a losing one is not that great. The guys don't get *really* excited until they get to the play-offs.'

Another game at home followed, against Philadelphia, and then the team flew to the West Coast, in its own charter plane, of course, staying in the very best of hotels, with each player having his own room and Gaze began to understand a little more of the situation he was in. He was in the company of serious professionals, to be sure.

And it wasn't just the totally earnest endeavour of their constant training. It was also in such things as their attitudes to groupies and drugs.

In the United States, groupies were there, 'hanging around the hotel lobbies and in the bars'.

'But as far as I could see, the guys were very good, and just weren't interested,' Gaze said.

'There was always a game coming up and there was simply no energy to be wasted on that sort of thing.'

Same thing with drugs . . .

'None that I could see,' said Gaze. 'One thing is that the NBA testing for recreational drugs is so strong, that you'd be crazy to take anything.'

(The NBA would have come up as dry as the Nullarbor if it had carried out a lifetime test to see if Gaze had *ever* tasted alcohol or nicotine. A strict teetotaller, he's never downed a cold one or taken a puff on a cigarette, let alone gone as far as try dope.)

'The other thing is, with over three hundred first-division college teams putting out fresh players every year, the supply of great players wanting your position is awesome, and if you want your million-dollar contract to keep flowing you've got to keep performing.'

The days passed. More training, more travelling, more video sessions, more analysis of the coming opponents, more games before huge crowds, then more strapping an aeroplane to his backside before moving on to the next town.

Gaze loved it, all of it. While others might have been daunted at such a life of never-ending basketball continuum, not him. He thrived. Thrived as if he was born to it . . . which, as a matter of fact, he was.

Back in Melbourne, from the first moments he had surfaced from babyhood to find himself as a toddler living in the little cottage that adjoins Albert Park Basketball Stadium, the constant background sound in his life has been of basketballs—*bop, bop, bop*—bouncing up and down on the gym floor, followed by *whooshka* as the ball went through the net. Every night, he went to sleep to that sound; every morning he woke to it.

He grew up in that same gym. Fooling around with basketballs all the while, being coached by his basketball coach father Lyndsay, respresenting Australia at the Olympics when he was only eighteen, captaining the Tigers to their first premiership last year (under his father's coaching), and turned himself bit by bit into one of Australia's most revered basketball champions along the way.

So, no, he was never going to get sick of the life of constant basketball with the Bullets. But after his second ten-day contract had expired, and some of Washington's regular stars were returning from injury, Gaze was thanked profusely for his efforts, told they would be in touch before the start of next season to see how things stood, and was given an air ticket home.

And now he's back. Relaxed, happy, booming with the good humour and the obvious satisfaction of one who's just lived his life's dream, albeit for only a short while, and full of stories of what it was like.

He tells them all in the warm-hearted and glowing way of

one who, in the extremely unlikely event he never achieves anything else with his life, is still assured of dying a happy man.

So, all up, what does it mean?

'It means I've been to the Show. I know what it's like and I've proved to myself that I can hold my own at that level,' he said.

'Maybe I'll be back there, and maybe I won't, but whatever else happens, I've been to the Show.'

He's been to the Show.

Mark Spitz

'I CALL IT the Mark Spitz Game Plan,' Norman Brokaw, Spitz's agent, said in 1972, soon after the American had won his seven gold medals at the Munich Olympics. 'My objective is to make an institutional tie-up for Mark very soon with two of the big blue-chip companies. Then I'm planning to work out two TV specials which Mark will star in during the 1972-73 season. After this, we're going to move heavily into the merchandising area worldwide. Then comes the personal appearance area. By the end of this year he will appear on two or three major shows . . . after this has been fully explored, we will approach the motion picture area, but not for at least six months. We feel that Mark Spitz will have a major motion picture career—I can see him playing the leading man in anything he does.'

Wow. And just to think that, twenty-one years later, the man himself will be coming into this very room any second now. They said he'd be here in a moment, and if only that accountant, or whoever he is, would move away from the door, a fellow could get a much better view of the great man arriving, and . . .

And hang on a sec. Surely that's not . . . please tell me he's not? You mean *this* is . . .

'Mark Spitz, pleased to meet you.' And pleased to meet you, too, Mr Spitz. (Small, really small, no moustache, no shoulders. Soberly dressed. Can one say without the *presence* you'd expect in someone who is, after all, one of the most accomplished athletes of the century?)

Of course, one doesn't actually expect the American to come through the door wearing red, white and blue swimmers with seven gold medals around his neck. Yet one is reminded of that image, anyway, when within ninety seconds of entering the room, Spitz is handing over two colour photographs of himself in just that classic pose. Sold four million posters of just this photo, he says in passing as he signs them.

The recipient, Joseph Walker—who won no less than nine gold medals for Australia, swimming in the recent Para-Olympics, is clearly delighted. As delighted as Spitz says he is to meet him.

'If I can touch somebody that becomes a better person through me talking to them,' he says afterwards, 'then I have sort of paid my debt back to my sport.'

Right. What does Spitz feel he gained from his own swimming career?

'I have such a great sense of accomplishment; not because I was so successful in winning all the gold medals but, more importantly, that I was successful in realising my own goals as a human being and as an athlete.'

Not to mention as a businessman.

No. Of course, all of the aforementioned deals didn't actually come through quite the way it was planned, 'because . . . they just didn't, that's all,' but he has moved onto other things, things like this terrific nutritional product he was here in Australia to promote. The same nutritional product that had helped him so much in his recent comeback attempt, of that he was quite sure. Even if it didn't in the end put him over the top and into the Barcelona Olympics it was a terrific product and a wonderful business to be involved in. And he wasn't just saying that, no sir.

So why had he been so successful in business where others have failed? Good question, says Spitz. *Great* question.

'My personal achievements in business have been directly attributable to the fact that I spent time on my education.' Not because his last name was Spitz and his first name was Mark?

Perhaps, initially, but 'if I was to change my name now and have cosmetic surgery, it wouldn't have any effect whatsoever on my business abilities'.

But seriously, whatever *did* happen to all those deals that were meant just to happen the way your agent Brokaw said they would?

'Well,' he says, looking a little defensive for the first time, 'they basically just didn't take off the way we thought they would and I went into other things . . . things like real estate.

'Things went very well for me in that business for a while,' he says ruminatively, though he refuses to be drawn on what went wrong after that.

Does he at least have some advice for Walker, who in his own way might face some of the same challenges that Spitz did?

Yes, yes, he does as a matter of a fact.

'Stay in swimming for as long as it gives you joy,' he says firmly, 'the longer the better. Don't be keen to rush off into other things while you're still getting pleasure from the pure act of swimming.'

Another round of handshakes and a couple more signed photos handed out, and he is gone again.

Blessed With Basic Instinct

IT WAS *THE* joke going around the Wallabies in mid-1991 . . . 'Have you read Campo's autobiography?' they would ask anyone who would listen. 'Wait till you hear the opening paragraph!'

Then they would begin to read, in suitably pompous tones:

'In that short, abbreviated hour between the fading of the winter's afternoon sun and the onset of that bitter night cold which persuades me that I could never live in the British Isles, I turned over in bed at a Surrey hotel where I was staying to take a telephone call which was to offer me the chance to change my life forever . . .'

The Wallabies' translation of what Campese had probably told his ghost-writer was slightly more succinct: 'Jeez, it was cold, and then the bloody telephone rang.'

Haw, haw, haw. How far from the true Campese style of address could the writer get? But if the biography wasn't of the type to give a true picture of the way the man is, none of the

Wallabies doubted that Campese's stature was such that he deserved that sort of attention. These days, as The Greatest Rugby Player Ever, Campese seems to get through life in aeroplanes, landing occasionally to play a match somewhere or other in the world—Australia, South Africa, Italy, Hong Kong, the British Isles et al—but it wasn't ever thus.

The first time I heard of him was in May 1982, just before the New South Wales Under-21 team took the field against the Canberra Under-21s when the New South Wales coach told us: 'Now watch out for this bloke Campese, I've heard he's dangerous.'

'Camp-*who*?' we said. Campese. We did go on to beat Canberra, but not before damn nigh every last one of us had made a fool of ourselves trying to bring this insolent fullback to ground.

Campese was soon selected for the senior Wallaby team to tour New Zealand under the coaching of Bob Dwyer.

'Are you nervous about facing Stu Wilson tomorrow?' the New Zealand journalists asked Campese before his debut in the first Test against the All Blacks.

'Who is Stu Wilson?' Campese asked. For the New Zealand journalists it was a moment of breathtaking arrogance, or stupidity, or *something*—but it defied belief that this young pup could not even know the name of the greatest winger New Zealand had produced, and the same one who would surely be burying him on the morrow.

With his first touch of the ball the following day, Campese stood Wilson up, and ran around him for a marvellous burst. He scored a try later in the game, also at the expense of Wilson and has since scored some sixty Test tries, played in another eighty-five Tests, enthralled crowds whenever he has played and constantly picked gaps others didn't even see. The most famous of these 'gaps' was surely the one that led to his try during the World Cup semi-final against New Zealand . . . How Campese determined it was possible to score such a try has been the subject of endless analysis.

The irony and wonder of it is best seen in the context of Dwyer's coaching philosophy. The First Commandment since he had first taken over the Wallabies had been 'Run straight'!

Yet, on this occasion, Campese broke every rule in the proverbial, running at almost a forty-five degree angle across the field, right under the guns of the momentarily mesmerised All Black defence. It seemed as if none of them could make out what on earth Campese was up to, perhaps each expecting the other to tackle him, and at the death, Campese was able to slice neatly inside the All Black winger John Kirwan for a try that would take Australia to a crucial 4-0 lead.

'*How* did he do that?' the rugby pundits wanted to know. '*Why* did he do it like that?'

Nick Farr-Jones, the Australian scrum-half, says: 'How does anybody even begin to try to analyse what Campese does? It always amuses me when people try to work out why Campese did this or that on a rugby field, when I'm sure not even David himself knows why he does it.

'It's an instinctive thing and David has been blessed because his instinct is one that is not only adventurous but it also seems to usually send him in the right direction at the right time. It's something you can't try to work out, you've just got to enjoy it.'

Which people do, of course, revelling in his offensive capabilities and forgiving him for his frequent defensive lapses. Come what may, they want to watch him play.

When at the end of the '91 World Cup, Campese suggested he was thinking of retiring, the Australian television network Channel Ten, which had just signed to broadcast rugby for three years, rightly saw that a lot of interest in Australian rugby would fall away with his departure and made him an offer he couldn't refuse.

If he continued to play for Australia for the next three years, they would employ him as a part-time rugby commentator at an annual salary of over $100,000. Put together with the prodigious sums he earns in Italy and the profits from the sports store he now owns in Sydney, Campese has some claim to being not only the best rugby player but also the best paid. Which is only fair.

Such is Campese's stature in the game now, he is the subject of endless word-portraits in many publications, and most of these invariably portray Campese as a generous, giving sort who has a charmingly frank way about him that can occasionally border on the acerbic, but only enough to add delightful spice to his character.

Hmmmm. Strictly speaking, this is not quite the way he is. Within the Wallabies, Campese is well respected for his abilities and admired for his totally professional attitude to training . . . but not particularly cherished as the man closest to the warm heart of the team. One with Campese's extravagant talents is always going to be a man apart within any side, but his apartness has been exacerbated by what Dwyer has described as 'a wire loose between his brain and his mouth'.

The reason, for example, I didn't actually get the man himself on the phone to write this piece is because we're not on warm terms any more. The cause was nothing too earth-shattering, just that I took exception to a few vicious things he once publicly and piously expressed about a Test brawl in which I was involved. As a matter of fact, it was in the same wretched autobiography I mentioned earlier.

Knowing Campese, I very much doubt if there was so much malice aforethought as a sudden acidic bubble coming to the surface at the wrong moment—as has happened many times before, and will no doubt happen again.

Many players over the years have been similarly burnt and share more or less my attitude: he is as marvellous an offensive rugby player as ever drew breath; he has in his career done rugby extremely proud and left it immeasurably richer for his passing; and he's as hard a worker for his success as ever we've met.

That he doesn't in the bargain also happen to be an engaging personality and loyal friend is regrettable. But what the hell. In the end, we're fairly glad he played the game.

Shane Warne

IT'S BEEN TEN DAYS now. Ten days, and here in Australia we still haven't come to the end of hearing about 'The Ball'.

You know the ball I mean. I'm talking, of course, about the first ball of Shane Warne's first over in the First Test of the Ashes at Old Trafford. I'm talking about the one where, after that superbly understated run-up by the fascinating blond bombshell, the ball left his wondrously talented arm to land with a telling bite of dust in front of the umpire at Square Leg before spinning fiercely to the left, to rise up and buzz around Mike Gatting's head a couple of times, all the while singing 'Advance Australia Fair' to further confuse him, before dropping right onto the stumps and knocking the bails back to their rightful position during any English innings— right on the ground at the base of the stumps. Howzat?

Not only *Out*, but something rather more than that. Let the Ashes series continue for another thousand years, and men and women will still say that this, *this* was the finest ball bowled—'The Ball of the Millennium'. In sum, this was the ball that conclusively demonstrated beyond all measure that though Australia has laboured long, she had at last given birth to the bowling equivalent of Sir Donald Bradman.

Or something like that. Actually, it did seem a rather goodish sort of delivery. And it really was interesting, the way Warne did it. Got the ball to spin, apparently, by dextrous use of his fingers and *that's* why it turned to the left like that to hit Gatting's wicket. Amazing.

More interestingly, though, has been the all but instant deification of Warne in Australia's popular imagination. In the time since he bowled it, his name and image have become apparent everywhere we look—on the television, in the newspapers, on T-shirts, on pages of magazines we see floating down the gutter. All of us now know more about 'That Ball' and Shane Warne's life than Switzerland knows about snow. When I turn on my radio—'. . .A *and in more news from the Australian team in England, Shane Warne*. . .'—he's there, too.

You get the drift. The question is *why*? Why such an immediate and overwhelming reaction?

Part of it is surely that just as nature abhors a vacuum, so, too, does a sporting nation like Australia hate to be without a real sporting hero on which to fasten its immense affections. Fact is, the country has been a bit light on for international sports heroes of late. Marathon runner Robert de Castella has retired, golfer Greg Norman seems lately more American than Australian, America's Cup sailor Alan Bond has gone bankrupt and our tennis players seem to thrash around only briefly on the court in Grand Slam events before being ushered to the exit. Enter, stage left, Shane Warne. All hail the conquering hero in a sporting contest that is, after all, the one we hold dearest to our hearts.

Warne's instant elevation may be further explained by the fact that it has been achieved in an old and mystical area of cricketing skill which we all thought had gone down with Atlantis. Many of us have heard about 'googlies', 'wrong 'uns', 'flippers' all our lives, without ever quite knowing what they were—quite simply because no-one was doing them anymore. Now, praise the Lord and pass the binoculars, an ancient art has been revived—an art which makes all other cricketing skills appear crass by comparison.

As one local writer put it, rather poetically, 'leg-spinners are the game's magicians, the fly fishermen in a world where others get their catch by tossing a stick of dynamite into a stocked dam'.

And to think that we used to worship at the altar of such unsubtle fast-bowling barbarians as Dennis Lillee and Jeff Thomson makes us all wonder what on earth we can have been thinking of.

Now, in Warne, we finally have a worthy heir to the three Australian spin greats of the past, the ones our fathers and grandfathers have often raved about—Bill O'Reilly, Clarrie Grimmett and Richie Benaud. Of course, after 'That Ball!', there can be no doubting that Warne is far and away the greatest of them, and that's one in the eye for our fathers. But as a minor matter of interest, each of the past three greats also used to hurl down their own 'Ball of the Century'.

As a case in point, Australian cricket writer Phillip Derriman recently dug up the account of a ball delivered by O'Reilly during the 1938 Test series in England which turned the Test on its own. As recounted by British writer Ralph Barker, English batsman Joe Hardstaff had been unwise enough to belt O'Reilly to the boundary for 2 fours in a row—the second off a no-ball—and O'Reilly was apparently so angry he could barely raise spit.

'With dramatic emphasis,' Barker wrote, 'O'Reilly paced out his run again, gesticulated fiercely, as though the call of a no-ball constituted a personal outrage and thundered up to the wicket to bowl the next ball. Like the girl in the novelette, O'Reilly was never more thrilling to watch than when he was angry. This time, he was livid with rage.

'No-one on the ground had seen a ball like it. It was the greatest ball O'Reilly ever bowled. It was not only fast, *really* fast, it was a vicious leg-break; Hardstaff sparred at it in bewildered fashion, and the ball just took the top of the the off-bail.'

Sounds just a tad like Warne's ball, doesn't it? OK, OK, so it didn't manage to sing the Australian national anthem as it hit, but still it wasn't bad.

Allan Border: Beyond Ten Thousand

IF YOU WERE to explain to an outsider what Allan Border has been all about for Australian cricket, what, in the end, would you say? Perhaps this: some are born great, others have greatness thrust upon them, and still others achieve greatness by batting on through the years. Tirelessly, unselfishly, *endlessly*. Batting on.

For Border, from the time he scored his first Test run against England at the Melbourne Cricket Ground in 1978 and batted on to his position now as the greatest Test run-scorer of all time, all we Australians have been rather distant admirers.

We like him well enough and have come to respect him greatly over the years, but in the end do not adore him the way we adored fast bowler Dennis Lillee, or stand in awe of him as we did Greg Chappell, or even *know* him like we feel we know Merv Hughes. He has just batted on without pausing, neither opening himself to the bowlers nor to us.

Part of it comes from the era in which Border has played.

When he started, in the time of Lillee, the nation's favourite poem went . . .

Ashes to Ashes,
Dust to dust,
If Lillee don't get 'em,
Thommo must.

Between Lillee, his fast-bowling partner Jeff Thomson, the great Greg Chappell and our favourite larrikin wicket-keeper Rod Marsh, there was little public affection left over for the bearded middle-order batsman from Sydney with the buttoned-down approach. But as the others all retired, or were injured or dropped, Border batted on.

When he was at the crease, flashy pull-shots for six were as rare as low scores from him. Most particularly when the situation was at its most dire, Border was the one who could be counted on to bat on, to put backbone back into the Australian innings. In his twenty-five Test centuries only three were scored in Tests won by Australia. Fifteen were scored in Tests that might well have been lost if Border hadn't batted on. Stoically, unselfishly, *constantly.*

In late 1984 the nation was rocked by the sight of the then Australian captain, Kim Hughes, resigning in a televised press conference, committing the unpardonable sin of *crying* as he did so. We Australians didn't mind our cricketing heroes hugging and kissing each other at the fall of every wicket, if they had to, but we'd be *damned* if we'd have a captain weeping in public.

Who could the nation turn to, and count on never to humiliate Australian manhood again? Allan Robert Border. We knew he'd bat on. Come what may.

And so it was. Border didn't cry once when Gower's English side beat Australia for the Ashes in 1985 and didn't cry again when the same side defended it successfully a year later. Didn't show much emotion at all, in fact. Just did his thing and batted on, our main saviour while all round him the Australian team crumbled.

David Gower went, and came and went again, but he at least paused long enough to captain the team beaten by Border's

Australian side 4-0 in the Ashes of '89. Was Border at least happy about this? Of course he was.

Mostly, though, he just batted on. Gower commented recently, without rancour, that 'it took me three months to get a sociable word out of him and even then it was only after Australia had wrapped the series up'.

That's our Allan, all right.

The nation has lived through 'interesting times' since. But in an increasingly uncertain world—with plagues, wars and economic uncertainty all around—there has remained the certainty that Border will get at least one half-century in any given Test. He's collected fifty-eight of them to date for a Test batting average of fifty-two.

And now here he is, sixteen years from his Test beginnings, the highest run-scorer of all time. Do we Australians take pause, and make ready to beat our breasts that we possess such a prodigy?

Not really. We take our cue from 'A.B.', as we are pleased to call him (not an affectionate nickname, but appropriately sober), and simply watch his coming retirement the way we might note the arrival of a train we are not catching.

In the end, we might wish that Border was a more excitable person, someone who could really be flashy and tell us something to *move* us. But if he'd been like that, if he'd been a man possessed of great and public passions, then in all probability he would not also be the man to do essentially the same thing, year in year out for sixteen solid years. So effectively. Without looking up.

What will he do when he eventually does retire?

Surely find another spot in the cricket world, and simply bat on, would be my guess.

A Different Sort of Man

WILLIE O REALLY DIDN'T WANT to stay for the after-match function, and neither did I. So a quick '*Look!*' to the left, as we ducked to the right, then through a door, out a window, down a fire escape, and we were out into the drizzly Wellington night.

And not a taxi to bless ourselves with. There was nothing for it but to walk back to the hotel, half an hour away. Trudging, trudging, trudging along.

So, who is this man beside me, anyway? What does anybody know about Willie Ofahengaue, other than that he's from Tonga, plays a football game straight out of hell, and is a very good and likable man? Willie doesn't give interviews and is excruciatingly embarrassed by his own fame. Given a choice, he would walk four blocks out of his way to avoid a single question from a journalist.

But this time, I had him. We had to walk thirty blocks together, and as I was cleverly disguised as a fellow footballer, there was nothing for him to do but to answer a few questions.

Did he enjoy the World Cup?

'Yes.'

Did he love playing for the Wallabies?

'Yes.'

Did he want to go to rugby league?

'No.'

Did he come across any racism when he was recently in South Africa?

'No.'

Trudging, trudging, trudging along.

No, it wasn't the stuff of which Pulitzer Prizes are made, but it was a start . . . and besides, that was at least four Willie quotes that, with his permission, I could put in a story—which was a lot more than most Willie profiles could claim.

Trudging, trudging.

Sometimes, surely, people must mistake Willie's reticence to speak for a lack of the smarts. It is not.

As a small example, there are more than ten possible moves than can be made from the back of the scrum in the New South Wales team. The rest of us have been trying to get them securely in our heads for the past four months. Only one player has never joined our discussion of them. Willie had them from the first moment he heard them. Never asked a question, never made a mistake.

Although these pre-planned moves go against the grain of the way he would prefer to operate—he admitted once, in a rare moment of verbosity, that he would prefer to 'just play'—it is enough that this is what the coach wants. No arguments from Willie.

And in the minute before going on to the field, the rest of us do all manner of things to get ourselves into a suitably aggressive frame of mind. We jump, sit, wave our arms, punch our palms—anything.

Willie prays. Not ostentatiously, so as you'd even notice—and it is not clear whether he prays for himself or the safety of his opposition—but that is what he does.

The rest of us sometimes get drunk, sometimes have smoked. Willie has done none of these things—ever. His strong Christianity forbids it. and for him that is the end of the section. Yet he never has even the slightest 'forbidding' air about him in the middle of our worst excesses.

Let it be, each to his own.

And how is it that Willie can be the most feared forward in the international game—featuring large in the nightmares of players from Auckland to Tokyo to London—yet has never raised an unprovoked fist in anger, or even engaged in mildly untoward rucking?

A different sort of man, to be sure.

The hotel is up ahead. Whaddya say we go to the bar and get smashed, Willie?

'No, Fitzy.' A small smile and a shake of the head.

Suddenly, in the back window of a parked van in front of the hotel pops up a little boy's smiling face. Then another, then another. Uncle Willie is back. Out of the small van comes an impossibly large number of people, Tongans all. In the middle of the throng, Willie turns and says: 'Family. See ya.'

See ya, Willie.

A different sort of man.

Nikki Lauda

HE'S RECOUNTED THE story so many times, its horror is told in the tone of a Sunday afternoon cup of tea.

'I was going down the straight at 280 kilometres an hour when something broke and I went straight into the wall and my car turned into a fireball and I was in there for fifty-five seconds at 800 degrees till they got me out and I was right on the point of death for days and I think I really did die once.'

Nikki Lauda, three-time world champion of Formula One racing, still bears souvenirs of that horrific crash in 1976.

Peeking out from under the cap he wears to cover a skull scorched bald, only half his left ear remains intact; Lauda is an obvious burns victim. Yet, somehow, Lauda is all humour and grace, with neither self-pity nor the hardness of someone who has had to overcome it. The crash wasn't any big deal, the way he tells it.

'I knew it was going to happen sometime,' he says, 'and I'm glad I survived it. But you don't begin to race if you're not prepared for it to happen.'

Of his near-death experience, he says: 'It was like falling into a big hole, and I just wanted to let go, to be sucked into this hole and just let go, let go. It was so nice. It was only when I realised this was what dying was that I shook it off and tried to wake up.'

Lauda kept awake from death by concentrating on every syllable the doctors were saying. Each syl . . . la . . . ble. Just keep away from the hole.

Three days later, he started to come out of immediate danger, and six weeks after that, incredibly, he was in Monza, Italy, heavily bandaged and preparing to race.

No, he says, he wasn't particularly courageous.

'I went out into practice that first day, and first gear was all right, but when I changed into second gear, I nearly s--- my pants. Really. I could not drive, I was just so scared.'

On the second day it was a bit better, and by the Sunday, Lauda was in fourth position on the grid. There was just one problem—no-one had told him that while he was in hospital they had changed the starting system from dropping the chequered flag to the current green-light system.

'I was sitting there wondering where the man with the flag was, when suddenly everybody around me was racing past, and from being fourth I went into the first turn at fifteenth.'

Lauda eventually fought his way back through the field to finish fourth. But he was back, and though he would miss winning that year's world championship by a point, he would go on to win two more world championships, bringing his total to a record three.

What he got out of it all, most notably, were money and fame. The money he put to good use in setting up Lauda Air, an international carrier which now boasts eight jumbos. The fame, he says, was good only to a point.

'It's terrific, at first, when you get your passport renewed in five minutes or can argue about a parking ticket and the police officer will let you go. But after a certain level, it's not good, people are always watching you. This I do not like.'

Some respite came last year, when Lauda visited the Boeing factory in Seattle to buy some more planes for his airline.

'They asked me, "Is Nikki or Lauda your surname?" and I

thought "Thank God, now this is my sort of place".'

Apart from money and fame, did Lauda not acquire some friends from his time in Formula One?

'None.'

None?

'It's just not like that. You're all against each other, on the track and off it. It's the nature of it.

'And even if you wanted to go and see another driver, you couldn't, because say you're with Marlboro and he's with Camel and if you're over in his pits and have your photo taken with Camel in the background, there are big, big problems. Some guys you talk to, like Piquet was one for me, but they're not "friends".'

Lauda lives with his wife and two children in Vienna and runs Lauda Air, which was for him the big challenge every sports person must look to when their sporting days are over.

'For racing, for any sport, you have to make sure you have a very strong alternative. Being at the top in your sport has big advantages, you live a competitive life, and make a lot of money, but at the end, what do you do? You are bored with the rest of your life if you don't go on to a bigger challenge.

'I see so many drivers now have to go down to the track and just hang around with the younger drivers to remember how it was, and I think this is very sad.

'For me, with Lauda Air, I'm in a new environment, which is bigger and more challenging, and I don't spend the second part of my life thinking about how good the first part was.'

Lauda is attending the Adelaide Grand Prix on Sunday in his capacity as an adviser to Ferrari. It was there, in 1985, that he competed in his last race.

'I didn't want to race, just did it because it said I had to in my contract. And there was a British Airways flight leaving to Europe halfway through the race, so I was praying my car would break early and I could catch the plane.

'But the car didn't stop, and I saw all the cars in front going so fast their tyres were breaking up, and suddenly I'm in the lead, so I think I may as well win it, and the hell with the plane. Eight laps before the end I touched the brakes and the car turned left into the wall and had a big smash—and that was that.'

All recounted with a wry smile.

Regrets, he's had a few—but, then again, too few to mention.

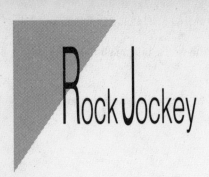

RockJockey

HALFWAY UP, I CONSIDERED my position. I was so scared, I was sweating bile, my fingers were bleeding from clawing the sheer Blue Mountains rockface, my toes were on a crag not big enough for a sparrow to be sick on and the only thing that kept me from oblivion on the rocks thirty metres below was a rope joined to the rock climber above me with whom I was having a serious personality clash. Or, at least, I would have been if he'd had a personality.

'Just move your right foot up a bit,' Rockhead was saying to me in his infuriating sing-song voice. 'There's another foothold just a *few* centimetres away! You can *do it*, I know you can!'

I hate people who always speak in exclamation marks and italics. And I was really hating Rockhead. So cheerful. So patiently patronising. Yet, as the most crucial link of my own lifeline, there was nothing I could do but more or less follow his instructions.

'There, I *told* you, you could do it! Well *done*, Peter, really well done!'

To hell with it. Perhaps if I grabbed his ankle and suddenly yanked hard I could have the satisfaction of seeing him tumbling downwards, downwards, ever downwards—and be able to unclip myself before the rope pulled taut, meaning I'd be alon . . . naaah.

The point of all this?

Exactly. That was what I was wondering.

Originally, it was to find the essence of this curious sport of rock climbing, discern what makes it the latest in the long line of thrill-seeking danger sports becoming so popular.

With hordes of 'rock jockeys' in the United States, Europe, Japan and Australasia rejoicing in it as their principal leisure pursuit, storming ashore and swarming over every vertical surface they can find, the question begs: Why?

Halfway up, it beat the hell out of me. But maybe the answer would come.

'Keep going, you're doing *well*! You're letting your feet do the thinking! Very goooooooood!'

I swear, I was gonna kill him. But even as we moved tortu-ously up the cliff, some vague sense of what the whole thing is about gradually came.

At the very least, your mind clears on the cliff something wonderful. All that clutter about mortgages and jobs and the fact that you only came third in last week's big ten-pin bowling competition are stripped away, and you're left only with a pressing need to survive and a few other stray thoughts that under normal circumstances would never be discerned amid the clutter, but which now register clearly.

Thirty metres from the top, for example, this thought sud-denly appeared in my head: How come in all the musical videos that have ever been done, with all those weird and wonderful themes ('Just to your right you'll find another foothold . . . well done!'), how come, I say, no-one has ever made a music video where this housewife is making coffee with a plunger, see, and through the kitchen window you can see this bridge in the background, and as she pushes the plunger down, the bridge explodes and falls into the river and . . .

And maybe it's just the adrenalin pumping through your

veins like a drug that keeps exposing these weird thoughts.

Now to the really difficult section. About three-quarters of the way up the cliff, the climbing path goes for about five metres on an angle of five past two on the clock face.

'Get your body *away* from the cliff!' Rockhead says.

You'd think that instinct would naturally press your body into a position best designed to climb. But no. While your overpowering impulse is to hug the cliff face, pressing your whole body up tight against the rock, to climb properly you apparently have to keep your bellybutton well out so as to improve your ability to move freely. Apparently, despite appearances, not even spiders have their bellies actually touching the wall.

Getting tired now, fingers getting sweaty, feeling slippery. Have these little crags ever had 125 kg hanging on them before? Which is a real worry when you're 130 kg. The abyss gapes, the chasm yawns, and worst of all, Rockhead is patronising me again.

'Your legs, your legs, your legs, your legs . . . let your *legs* do the work!'

But he's right. The trick is to let your legs bear all the weight, and do all the work whenever possible. Although expert climbers are apparently able to lift their own body-weights just on the strength in their fingers, the general rule is that the legs are the engine and the fingers the steering wheel.

The worst thing about the last fifteen metres is having to listen to Rockhead's continued blandishments about how terrific the view is at the top; how he's never seen someone climb so well on their first go!; how I'd be so exhilarated when I got to the summit!; and on and on into the ever et cetera, always with those infernal exclamation marks at the end of everything he said.

Yet, even through the momentary confusion of wondering whether, when I got to the summit, it would be better to push him from the top or just hold him out by his ankles over the cliff, I really did get a rush of pleasure when I got to the top . . . of splendid isolation . . . of uniqueness—all the rest of the world is getting by on the humdrum horizontal axis, while it seems that only Rockhead and I are working on the verily vertical. Making us feel very special, indeed.

See, *anybody* can proceed on a flat surface, only we can do it the hard way, as we force nature to cede to our will, for we are not ordinary men . . . and all that sort of stuff.

I suppose with most climbers it would be enough to make you feel a special bond with the person you're climbing with. I can't say that that actually happened this time, but at least I let Rockhead live.

Rallying to Cause of Driver Speeding Towards Insanity

FLY DOWN TO THE nation's capital, they said. You'll have a terrific time, they said. In the car with the fastest rally driver ever, they said.

A blur of movement, a thrashing of the gears, the slightest touch on the brakes, then—with the hint of a maniacal laugh—a hard stamp on the accelerator and we shot through the gap, straight out of the airport car park . . . The rally PR lady turned out to be a genuine devotee of the sport, too.

'Possum' Bourne, she said, was one of the most successful rally drivers the nation had ever known, with easily the best car ever, she said, a four-wheel-drive Subaru, she said . . . that's S-U-B-A-R-U, she said.

PR people are like that. Blah, blah, blah.

But, thankfully, here is Possum now, standing in a clearing in the forest. Smooth-looking sort of fellow, moustache, bespectacled, friendly—surprisingly normal-looking for a man who will in short order turn out to be a card-carrying lunatic.

And there's the car, $350,000 worth of machinery and not

even a decent stereo system. Instead, it's all buttons and dials and computer screens and bare, stripped metal. According to my notes, Possum said the car had a *'something* carburettor *something-something* with double overhead quad-cam and stripped back *something-something* turbo'. Meaning, I gathered, that it was a hellava fast car.

But time to rock 'n' roll. Into the bucket seat. Me and my mate Possum. Helmet? Check. Left seatbelt? Check. Right seatbelt? Check. Waist seatbelt? Check. Nappy for the passenger? Very funny.

So anyway, uh, Possum, how did you come by that nickname?

'Rolled my mum's car when I was fifteen to avoid hitting a possum.'

And you'll just be making idle chit-chat like that, and Possum'll be recounting how his own expression for 'going flat out' is 'giving it death' when out of the corner of your eye you'll see a man holding a small flag on a stick above his head.

And you'll be just saying, 'Uh, Possum, what's the man doing with the fla . . . ,' when the man suddenly drops the flag and Possum emits a kind of animal grunt and goes certifiable for the first time.

Your helmeted head hits the backrest, and bounces back to the vision of a solid pine tree coming at you at 160 km/h. Then, at the last moment, he swings left so as to go over a cliff instead, but again changes his mind and decides it might be even more fun to smash right into a huge boulder at the side of the road, but then again what say we absolutely obliterate ourselves by smashing at 150 km/h into that stone culvert, or maybe it would be even better to go so fast into this corner that we roll over and over and kill ourselves that way?

On and on like this. Kilometre after kilometre of this circuit, with him betraying no visible emotion and me feeling like I did one wet Wednesday night when the back of my MGB slid out going around a corner and for the barest moment I thought I was going to slide under an oncoming garbage truck and die dead dead dead as a dodo bird. Maybe as dead as two dead dodos.

But *then* I felt that terror for just the barest moment, and *now* I'm feeling it for five minutes straight, and I wonder if I can stop this macho posturing of trying to appear nonchalant and unconcerned and instead grab this suicidal mongrel dog by the throat and yell at him: 'Will you stop this bloody #$%^&*! car, Possum, or do you want me to *tear your $%^&* throat out!?!*'

No kidding! To say that he drove the car 'fast' is only to state the bleeding obvious. It is *how* fast he drove it that counts.

At any given moment he was driving it about 1 km/h slower than a terrible accident. It's like Graham Hill wrote in his book *Life at the Limit*, 'the ultimate thrill comes when the car is at its limit in the corner; one per cent faster and you crash, one per cent slower and you lose the race'.

Luckily, you remember that quote through your terror and you start to get a grip. You realise this is just the business of rally driving. The skill of the game is to always be right on the edge of losing control without ever quite getting there. What makes my good mate Possum one of the best is that he can judge that point more accurately than most, and is quite comfortable sitting there. While *you* might be as scared as a porcupine trespassing in a balloon factory, Bourne has been living in the same balloon factory for so long he pays rent.

None of this makes him any less a lunatic for his crazy passion. But it is comforting, for all that. The only real panic you feel after that is soon afterwards, back at the airport, when you know for sure the plane is going too slow to take off.

episode occurred which brought home to me that, while it is nice to escape from one's comfortable middle-class existence and take a walk on the seamy side every now and then, this seamy side also has a cutting edge which can be dangerous.

Our reunion had been in progress for a couple of hours and we had given out the usual quota of cigarettes and small amounts of money to those who asked, when we were approached by one of the group of Spanish *punkis* (punks in English) that also haunt the place.

The first emissary was a *punki* girl to whom we gave a cigarette. It was when we demurred at letting her keep the silver cigarette lighter she'd used to light it that the trouble started. Taking umbrage at our reticence, the chief *punki* came over and menacingly demanded that we give his girlfriend the lighter. Still we refused, with me as chief spokesman, and it was at this point that a big glob of spit emerged from the chief *punki*'s mouth, traced a perfect arc, and landed right on my shirt.

Is there anything more insulting and infuriating in this world than being spat upon?

Desperately trying to keep my cool I wiped it off with a napkin and tried to reason with the guy. But when, after more remonstrations, the second glob landed, I exploded and we ended up in a dead sprint back to the hotel being pursued by twenty enraged *punkis*—the chief spitter of whom was now bleeding from his insolent mouth.

We only just made it back in time to lock the door and keep the angry mob out.

Acting instinctively, we menfolk turned the tables over to use as barricades on the windows and took up our position behind them while the womenfolk busied themselves reloading our rifles and tending to the wounded. No, only kidding. But for a while there it really did seem like a situation out of the Wild West as seemingly every punk in the area started to mill around the front door shouting and throwing things up at our windows. Fortunately the cops eventually came in response to the manager's call and the whole situation was calmed down.

Nevertheless, it did my nerves no good the next morning to read scrawled into the pavement in chalk, '*MUERTE A EL*

GRANDE' (death to the big one) and for the next three days I was, to say the least, very circumspect when within coo-ee of the brutes.

For all that though, the magnetism of the place still holds sway on me and I usually wind up back there at least once every six months.

We Wuz Robbed in Unfair Fight of Force and Farce

IT WAS A BIT OF concrete, near an old smokestack, on the roof of the building where I work.

And it was a worry all right. No matter that he doubled my age, that I doubled his weight and stood a good three heads taller to boot. The problem was the difference in the length of our credentials. In the blue corner, Peter Fitz, hailing from the West, an ageing footballer with only a little experience in the odd on-field brawl.

And in the red corner, Master Wu of Taiwan, from the East—son of the famous warrior Wu Kuochung, student of even more famous warrior Cheng Man-Ch'ing, receiver of many awards for valour in battle from Chiang Kai-shek himself, and president of the International Tai Chi Association to boot. And that was the good part. The bad part was that Master Wu's advance publicity had suggested that, by his mere touch, he would be able to take my internal energy, add it to his own and somehow be able to flick me backwards two metres into the wall. Like magic.

But let's leave our two warriors for a moment as they circle each other warily.

The problem with a lot of these Eastern arts for us Westerners is that we have an in-built desire to discount them. The further you go into them, the more the suspicion grows that you are nought but a pasty white Westerner, kind of buffalo-ing your way through life, while these inscrutable Easterners are able to call on all the mystique and unknowable things of their land.

We go to McDonald's while they go to the temple sort-of-thing. The fear is that, if you go on with it, you might end up atop some mountain range eating wheatgrains and studying under some guru.

But back to the circlers . . .

So we came to grips. Oddly, and most disappointingly, no explosion. I was not blasted against yonder wall at his mere touch and nor did I feel any magical powers upon me. Not even the jolt of anything slightly mystical or other-worldly. Apparently, this was because I was too heavy and not angry enough, but we'll come to that.

For the moment, I was at least left in no doubt that if we had been engaged in a serious fight instead of a mock one, I would have lasted about five seconds before being left broken and bleeding on the ground.

If I would punch at his head, he would dodge and strike back before I had even time to draw my fist back. If I chanced to get a meaningful grip on his throat, he, with only minimal pressure, pressed somewhere on my wrist and made me release. He could send a foot flicking past either of my ears at will.

A French rugby forward might arguably be just as physically tough, but the difference was that Master Wu's own fighting knowledge was based not on ten years of football, so much as some 2500 years of learning by his forebears . . .

After it was all over, the cleaners were trying to collect the pieces and mop me up. The Master was at pains to point out that tai chi is not merely a martial art, so much as a philosophy and a way of life. After all, all those people you sometimes see in the park making like a stork as they stand on one leg doing all those weird movements are also practising tai chi, and their aspect is obviously one of great calm.

As near as this hopelessly addled Western mind can grasp, the martial-art aspect of tai chi is part of the philosophy that all things are guided by the need for equilibrium between the forces of 'yin' and 'yang' and the overload of yang on our part, which is anger, can be converted by him, the master of yin, into power that he is able to use against us.

It sounds impressive, all that last bit, doesn't it? I mean 'yin' and 'yang' and all that sort of stuff. Personally, I really wanted to believe it—or at least to be shown that, apart from being an obviously superb fighter, there really was some force Master Wu could call on that could have, as promised, blown me backwards into the wall.

The pain of my bruises would have been countered by the knowledge that the force existed, as advertised, and that I had personally been blown away by it.

But not a bit of it. I simply received a knees-up-Mother-Brown thrashing from a very skilled fighter. But no 'magic', dammit, which was the reason I'd agreed to be beaten up by him in the first place. Maybe I'm being unfair, and maybe it was, as Master Wu's PR guy explained, that you had to be a lot more inscrutable than me to get it really; that tai chi as a martial art is not an offensive force but a purely defensive one that can only be activated against an offensive one. Or something like that . . .

Telling it to Him Straight

SMOOTH. VERY SMOOTH. 'Peter, mate,' he said, 'I've got a business proposition I'd like to make you.' A business proposition? A *business proposition*?

You mean, a proposition like Bondy and Skasey and Holmes à Courty were always involved in, before the last died and the first two went bust? OK, not a happy ending for any of them, but for the sort of money those guys pulled down, one could stand a little unhappiness at the end of the line. Right? Right.

'Sure,' I said equally smoothly, sort of deathly calm-like, as I tried to contain my rising excitement. 'What's your business proposition?'

'I'd rather not say too much now,' Reggie said, as he looked nervously around him. 'But maybe I can come see you at your home on Saturday morning . . . ?'

Of course. Whatever his proposition was, it was obviously a biggie, obviously something that might enable a poor working stiff like me to break out of wage-slavery at a single stroke and get into the really Big Bucks. No matter that I didn't know this friend of mine had any business background of note—if he wanted to see me in my house, on a Saturday morning, he obviously had something of moment to impart, and the very least I could do was hear him out.

'Now,' Reggie said, tapping with his deconstructible pointer on the deconstructible blackboard he'd just set up in my livingroom, 'did you ever think about you . . . your place in the world, and the sort of deal you're getting from it? Did you ever think you wanted more?'

The first terrible suspicion hit me. Disguised as my friend, sort of, Reggie was now revealing himself as the representative of some whacko religious sect that wanted me to give my life and property over to God or somesuch. This, in his whacko way of thinking, would be good business, as I'd give God all my worldly goods and in return God would give me eternal life. Cheap at the price, he no doubt thought.

But nooo. Reggie denied my first bitter accusations and continued.

'Tell me, Pete, mate, did you ever think about the middle-man?' (*No.*)

'Did you ever think about how much of the money you spend on detergent gets wasted on people that aren't the manufacturer?' (*Not once.*)

'Well, did you ever think you'd like to make a lot of money?' (*Yes! Now* you're getting warmer, Reggie. I never think of anything else.)

'Ever hear of Amway, Pete, mate?'

Hold it. Hold it right there. Where's my mace? You're wasting your time, Reggie, and far more importantly, you're wasting *my* time.

Reggie went kicking and screaming all the way, digging his heels into the carpet and holding the leg of the kitchen table as he kept howling that if I'd only listen to him, half the known universe would come into my possession for practically no effort on my part, and he knew people that started only three years ago and already they drove Rolls Royces and if only I listened I could be a Platinum or an Emerald or something which meant that I'd be making hundreds of thousands of dollars every month just by selling household goods to my friends and, and, and, and (*clunk*). Thank God, I finally got the mongrel out and the door closed—even if I did have to slam the door a few times on his fingers to do it.

'Think about it!' were his final screamed words to me.

(*Time passes.*)

Listen Reggie, you knucklehead, I *have* been thinking about this, and have even talked to a few of my other friends about it. They, too, have been approached at one time or another by the Amway crowd, and had the same gut reaction as mine. But because we were all approached by friends or pseudo-friends, none of us ever really got round to enunciating what exactly it is that gets our goat about this system of selling, and your way of trying to rope us into it.

But enough is enough. For future reference, Reggie et al, listed below are a few points which, no doubt, hundreds of people want to make to you, but have been prevented by politeness from doing so:

1. We resent you using friendship as your primary marketing tool in snaring our business.
2. We resent you hiding the crucial word 'Amway' so far into your spiel that we are all well up the garden path before realising we've come to a dead end. If you must do this sort of stuff then it is surely courtesy to a 'friend' to tell them what you're on about before the whole thing begins.
3. As to the actual selling of the stuff . . . you can call us old-fashioned if you like, but we retain the idea that friends are friends, detergent is detergent, and ne'er the twain shall meet.
4. We have better things to do with our time than to spend Saturday mornings going around spreading the word of Amway. Sure, we all vaguely want to be millionaires—but only in the manner that, as five year olds, we all wanted to be generals, pilots and prime ministers. You grow out of it. Or, at least, most of us do.
5. Couldn't you try selling the stuff to each other in a sort of

circular fashion? That way, if we're lucky, you could just run around in ever-diminishing circles until you eventually disappear up each other's backsides, to leave the rest of us in peace.

If it Wasn't For Golf...

THEY'RE A CURIOUS breed. In the name of 'leisure', they like to move around in small bands thrashing tiny balls with big sticks. All over the planet—up hills, down dales, over waters, through forests, out of sandpiles, and every now and then into tiny holes. Cursing all the way, speaking the gobbledegook of a dead language, with their 'bogeys' and 'niblicks', 'birdies' and 'eagles' ever aflutter. And traditionally wearing absurdly striped pants and shirts that desperately need their volumes turned down, endlessly muttering about wicked fate that has once again denied them the score they so richly deserved.

The two bored Scottish shepherds who started all this all those moons ago have a lot to answer for. If one lazy afternoon when the sheep were quiet, those two Celtic wretches hadn't decided to pass the time by whacking some small rocks down a couple of rabbit burrows with their crooks, the world as we know it would be entirely different.

Our summer TV screens would not be clogged with infernal

images of the weird ones doing their stuff; huge tracts of land all over the world would not be eternally prissied, preened and greened; many of our closest friends wouldn't spend vast amounts of their time playing golf, watching golf and talking about the time they hit this faaa-bulous approach shot on the tenth fairway of Royal Sydney, choosing a five-iron to drive into the gusty westward wind, see, and dropping their left shoulder just right at the last instant, as they caressed the ball to send it soaring away to the far horizons and you should have seen how . . . *suddenly you are getting sleepy . . . very sleepy . . .*

If it wasn't for golf, political leaders worldwide would be entirely bereft of wonderful photo opportunities to give them that oh so crucial JFK 'look'. While racing may be the sport of kings, it is golf which is the sport of prime ministers and presidents—and no heads of state worthy of the name (with the notable exception of our own Paul Keating, *bien sur*) don't at least occasionally head out on to the links with another head of state as the cameras whir and purr. Sometimes the way these political leaders hit their shots can set the tone of their entire government.

On the first vacation of his presidency, George Bush drove hard off the first tee, and the *New York Times* dutifully recorded his words: 'Oh, golly darn, get up there!' Four years later they were there again, this time to record President Clinton's immortal mutterings in exactly the same situation: 'Whoa, mama, stay up!' Which says it all: the patrician and the beatnik.

Business, too, is equally rotten through and through with golfing passion.

'Corporate golf days'—where the pinstripe patrol takes its best clients out on to the links for a day and very carefully just manages to lose to them—are to the nineties what Filofaxes were to the eighties. Everywhere and always, the corporate tool to beat them all. *None* of them are immune.

Not even other sportsmen are immune. You'd think, wouldn't you, that former Wallaby captain Nick Farr-Jones' fondest memory of the last few years would be when he was minding his own business walking along one day, and reached above his head for the hell of it, only to come down with the Rugby World Cup, handed to him by the Queen of England. But not a bit of it.

'It was out on the sixteenth,' he recounts, 'at the Lakes Course, playing in a Pro Am, going straight into a stiff breeze and I was playing with Brett Ogle. I decided to use a three-iron (*this shouldn't take too much longer if I can just hurry him up a bit*) and instead of caressing the ball like you're meant to, I just really hit as hard as I could and *connected*, drilling it right up the fairway (*fascinating . . . any chance we could get to the point here?*), it started on a low trajectory and just kept rising, before dropping out of the skies about five metres from the pin (*this makes 'Days of our Lives' look like a news flash*). Unfortunately, I went on to make a bogey from there, as putting is not my forte, but that shot was my best ever.'

Great, and remind me never to ask you again.

Look, it gets worse. Other countries have military leaders who like nothing better than the smell of napalm in the morning, who spend all their time planning how to kill the maximum number of people most efficiently, like military leaders should.

Not us. Our most powerful military figure, the chief of the defence force, Admiral Alan Beaumont, likes to get out on the golf course and shoot a few holes. His staff says that's where he 'does a lot of his thinking'. Terrific.

The problem is not, of course, just how widely spread the game is, how insidiously it has penetrated all strata of society, it is most particularly the sort of people it helps produce . . .

Golfers are, by nature, a precious bunch. Who cannot recognise, for example, the following P.G. Wodehouse description in every golfer they know?

'The least thing upsets him on the links. He misses short putts, because of the uproar of the butterflies in adjoining meadows.'

Prima donnas all, the only thing admirable in the whole sorry saga is that golfers generally recognise all too well the depths of their common affliction and like nothing better when the day is done than to sit around the clubhouse and tell golfing stories, the common theme of which is what frightful nutters they really are—ever consumed by the same unreasonable urge to play golf, come what may.

Take old Smithers, for example. Why only last Wednesday, they say, the old fellow was out on the links for his regular round with young Barnaby Smythe-Jones and the youngster was most moved to see Smithers pause in his putt as a funeral cortege passed by on a nearby road, take off his hat, and observe a minute's silence.

'How very decent of you, to be so respectful 'n' all!' cried the youngster when the old man had resumed his stance.

'I think it only right,' growled Smithers soberly in reply. 'We'd been married nearly forty years.'

Haw, haw, haw. But golfers love those sort of stories, the better to illustrate just how many sandwiches short of a picnic they really are.

For the rest of us, though, the whole thing is getting beyond a joke. Unless something is done soon to curb their outrageous and insidious enthusiasm, the world as we know it risks becoming one big golf course, with the deserts as sand traps and the seven mighty oceans reduced simply to being big water obstacles.

No kidding. The situation is now dire enough that last September saw the world's first World No-Golf Day, organised by Gen and Nana Morita, the co-founders of the Global Network for Anti-Golf Course Action. (Like, where do I sign?)

According to the *Earth Island Journal*, there are currently 24,000 golf courses on earth of which 13,000 are in the United States. Which means, of course, that all up, there are now 2.3 million hectares of the planet's surface taken up with golf courses, and that figure is growing by as much as 120,000 hectares a year. (So now we know where the rainforests are going.)

The green peril—spreading to all corners of the globe in the coming decades—is every bit as threatening as the Red Menace was in past decades. This time, though, we, the people, will not be able to rely on a politically guided military–industrial complex to get together and do something to stop it—for all three tiers of that powerful junta are completely rotten with golfing freaks.

No. This time, it is going to require genuine people-power—an outright refusal by the entire populace to pick up a golf club for anything other than beating around the head and shoulders anyone telling a golfing story, would be a good start.

The Anzac Cricketers

IT WAS UNDOUBTEDLY the most extraordinary game of cricket ever played. History records not a jot of who batted, bowled or fielded, nor even whether there was a result, but its uniqueness relies nought on something so trivial as the score. It was where it was played that counts, and under what circumstances. Gallipoli, December 1915. The battle had been lost, the struggle forgone. Britain's General Kitchener gave the orders to pull the Anzacs out and send them on to the Western Front in France.

Under cover of darkness, the evacuation began on 8 December. Over the next eleven nights, 35,445 men were safely evacuated onto the ships, suffering only one minor casualty in the process.

As the ranks began to noticeably thin, it was decided something should be done to alleviate whatever suspicions Johnny Turk might be harbouring about the decreased activity. The orders went out from First Division Command that each battalion was to be as active as possible within sight of the

Turks, to create the impression that these visible men were the 'tip of the iceberg' of the troops still in the trenches (many of whom had since departed). Each battalion was to interpret these commands as it saw fit. Many chose to have men loitering about, gazing at the sky, just beyond the range of the enemy guns.

Some men from New South Wales 4th Battalion had different ideas. Why not a cricket game? (Apart from the inconvenience of mortar and rifle fire from the trenches above, that is.)

The relationship between the Turks and the Anzacs had evolved by this time to the point where taking potshots at distant figures was not absolutely automatic; but on the other hand, the departing hospital ships were full of diggers who had trusted this line of reasoning too far.

It was a tentative group, therefore, who, on the afternoon of 17 December 1915, took to the pockmarked patch of ground known as Shell Green (so named because it was under permanent Turkish artillery fire). The Turks in the trenches above must have wondered what on earth was going on as the game started. Was this grenade-throwing practice? Or perhaps a method of whacking incoming grenades back to the far trenches from whence they came?

Who knows what they thought, but for the first two hours of the game the Turks held their fire and watched.

'But after two or three hours the Turks had had enough of this strange spectacle,' says Australian war historian Bill Gammage, 'and started to send down some mortar fire to clear the Australians out. The Turks probably still didn't know what was happening, but wanted whatever it was stopped.'

Did the mortar fire stop the cricket cold? Not a bit of it. According to the diary of one Granville Ryrie, the game continued regardless, 'just to let them see we were quite unconcerned . . . and when shells whistled by, we pretended to field them. The men were wonderfully cheerful and seemed to take the whole thing as a huge joke.'

Another account of the game, courtesy of the Australian War Memorial, says 'the shrapnel cut and hissed across the pitch and the outfield, and there was as great a risk of lost life as a lost ball'.

When the Australians still didn't retire, the Turks unleashed doubly heavy salvos of mortar fire and, in the end, 'the Australians reluctantly called it a draw and retired to tea'. Happily, there is no record of any player having to 'retire hurt', or worse, during the game.

Two days later, all players were safely evacuated to either be killed on the fields of France or to survive and make it home, home to Australia.

Shell Green now serves as a cemetery for fallen Anzacs.

When England Won the Test Series 3-0

IT WAS ANOTHER TIME, another place . . .

After the Japanese invaded Malaya in December 1941 and pushed on down to capture Singapore the following February, many of the trapped Allied troops had to surrender. They were rounded up and forced to march to Changi, on the eastern tip of Singapore Island, where they were obliged at gunpoint to labour long in aid of the Japanese war effort.

In one part of Changi, in a place called the Serangoon Road Camp, remnants of the scattered Australian Imperial Forces were in the same compound as the Royal Norfolk Regiment of Britain. Initially, there was little contact between these two groups, which had been assigned different work details and slept in their own barracks.

One Australian who was there, Lieutenant Richard Conway, now seventy-eight and living in Australia's capital, Canberra, remembers the situation well: 'They were extremely tough times and there was no time for socialising, yet every three weeks or so, the Japanese would announce, "*ashita yasumi dessu*" or "holiday tomorrow". On these occasions a few of us Australians would often play a rough game of cricket in the middle of the clay compound.'

It was on one of those days, in August 1942, when the Australians were 'just mucking around with an old bat and ball', that two officers of the Norfolk Regiment wandered over to watch them perform and began chatting to Conway.

'Such is the charm of cricket,' Conway recounts, 'that presently we were talking like we'd all been friends all our lives and we began yarning about the controversial Bodyline series of ten years before. They, of course, thought Bodyline wasn't a bad idea at all . . .'

That friendly argument aside, the two Englishmen were most impressed to learn that back in Sydney, Conway had been a member of the first-grade Waverley side and had actually played with the great Alan Kippax, the Australian Test player of the time whom the English apparently regarded as an even better strokemaker than Bradman.

Soon afterwards, one of the British officers, Lieutenant L. W. Curtis, hailed Conway and informed him that on the next *yasumi*, the English would like to play a 'Test match' against the Australians in the compound.

Conway replied that 'we might struggle to come up with a team, but Curtis said, "Wherever you find a body of Australians, you'll have no trouble getting a cricket team together". And he was right.'

When Conway informed the Australians of the English challenge, he was greeted with great enthusiasm and Conway himself was appointed captain 'basically because I'd played with Kippax'.

The coming match became the talk of all the POWs, and the next *yasumi* day was awaited with eager anticipation. On a Saturday three weeks later, the Japanese announced the next day was to be a rest day and the match was on. It had been decided that this first Test match would be designated as taking place at 'Sydney', where the 1940 Ashes first Test would have taken place had the war not intervened. One innings for each side, and the game would be wrapped up in a day.

On the eve of the match, Conway was amazed to be handed by the English officers a carefully typed list, setting out the English team members, the umpire and the scorer, and informing the Australians that the wicket would be 'pitched at ten-thirty am'.

'It was typically British, that sort of formality,' Conway said. 'But I just couldn't figure out where they got the typewriter from.'

He was to be even more surprised the next day when he and his teammates turned up in their 'rough and ragged shorts and thongs' to find the English 'extremely well turned out in their Bombay bloomers'.

Not only that, but somehow the Brits had come up with a full canvas cricket kit, with stumps, pads, bats and a new six-stitcher ball.

The Australian team was staggered.

'With this regiment,' Conway said, 'cricket was a very big thing, and they told us that even through the whole retreat, surrender and forced march to this camp, they had still managed to keep this cricket kit intact. It was extraordinary!'

But to the game. The clay pitch had been stamped down beautifully by the Brits, and was very playable, 'giving a reasonably even bounce'. The boundaries were a combination of barracks and barbed wire.

For men living on only eight grams of rice a day, worked endlessly and ravaged by dysentery, various skin diseases, Singapore foot and the dreadful *beri-beri*, it was not easy to play a full-blown cricket match, but the way Conway tells it, this was different.

'All of us, Australians and Brits, had always dreamed since we were little boys of playing cricket for our countries, and this was it,' he said. 'Our POW status didn't exist and we were prisoners no longer. It was a Test match between England and Australia and that was it. All of us forgot everything else. We were playing for *Australia*.'

The match, however, was almost over before it had begun. With Australia batting first, the ball at one stage eluded the English wicketkeeper, Lieutenant-Colonel E.C. Prattley, and ran down under the coiled barbed wire fence to the feet of a gigantic Sikh who was guarding them. With Singapore's fall, many of the Sikhs had changed sides to the Japanese. This fellow refused to give them back the ball.

'We Australians thought that was the end of the match,' Conway recounts. 'But the Brits would not have a bit of it. Not a bit deterred, Colonel Prattley, still with his pads on, left his post behind the stumps and marched determinedly with his adjutant to the Japanese guardroom.

'In a matter of minutes, they re-emerged with the commanding officer of the guards, a little bloke by the name of Corporal Jita, and together they all marched straight towards this big bearded Sikh, who looked about eight foot tall with his turban.'

Then the denouement.

'Jita shouted at the Sikh and then without further ado landed on the Sikh's jaw a wonderful uppercut that would have done justice to Joe Louis, and dropped him to the ground. Jita then picked up the ball, gave it to Colonel Prattley and marched straight back to the guardhouse.'

The Anglo-Australian Test continued. The Australians fought valiantly, but as the day wore on, the weight of England's superior batting and bowling expertise eventually carried the match for them and the upshot, in the words of Conway, was that 'we got clobbered'.

And they were clobbered in another two Tests in 'Brisbane' and 'Melbourne' over the next six weeks on successive *yasumis*. The star of the English side was Geoff Edrich (brother of the England international Bill Edrich), who scored three successive hundreds against the Australians.

The brute.

The Tests broke up in late 1942 when many of the POWs were sent to other camps, and other work details in different parts of Asia. Lieutenant Conway was sent to the Thai-Burma Railway, had a tough time but survived to tell the tale.

He is the only survivor on the Australian side.

Yabba the Barracker

HE WAS FROM a time when, to judge by the photos, Sydney Town was coloured exclusively in black and white; when most men wore hats and women wore long skirts; when the sure-fire pinnacle of the sporting season was Australia playing a Test match at the Sydney Cricket Ground.

And at such matches it was one 'Yabba' who stood tallest, boomed loudest and most dominated off-field proceedings for four decades. The Test players would come and go as the seasons passed, the umpires would change every five years or so, but Yabba, the 'World's Greatest Living Barracker', was seemingly eternal.

Born Stephen Gascoigne, Yabba was raised on the mean streets of Redfern and worked as a rabbitor around Balmain. His fame extended throughout the cricketing world—so much so that even the imperious English captains were known to seek out Yabba and shake hands with him before a Test match.

Standing on the Hill beneath the spot where the old scoreboard still stands, Yabba's booming voice would roll across the ground like a tide—'Have a go, ya mug!', 'Look out, umpire, he's gone mad!', 'Come on, you drongos!'—engulfing all. Some of Yabba's shouted sayings went on to earn a place in the Australian vernacular, but it was said he was at his immortal best when firing off spontaneous witticisms.

Once, for example, when the two great English batsmen Jack Hobbs and Percy Sutcliffe had both passed the century and looked like batting all day, the Australian captain brought on the last of his bowlers in a final attempt to break the partnership. From his stronghold on The Hill, Yabba proffered this advice, in a voice that would drown out thunder: 'It's no use, skipper— you'll have to get the fire brigade to put them out.'

Even the umpires roared with laughter, so the story goes.

The great Tiger O'Reilly recalls an incident in the 1930s when the Sydney umpire George Barwick had his hand up in the air for a prolonged period as he signalled a groundsman to move the sight-board to the batsmen's satisfaction. Barwick had just about accomplished his purpose when Yabba could brook the delay no longer.

'It's no use, George,' he cried, 'teacher hasn't seen you— you'll have to wait for playtime.'

To Yabba must also go the credit for originating the immortal message 'Git a bag'—advice he flung from the Hill to awkward fielders in the arena who missed catching out a batsman or failed to stop a ball on its way to the boundary. Some dusty footage which surfaced recently from deep in Channel Nine's archives actually shows Yabba in 1936 delivering this last line as 'Gidddddabaaagg'. The drawling delivery splits his big Australian face for as long as two seconds.

When Hanson Carter, the Australian wicketkeeper who worked as an undertaker, caught Hobbs, Yabba exclaimed from The Hill: 'You can take the body away now, Hanson!' Possibly a case of 'You had to be there', but there is no doubting the affection in which Yabba was held at the time, both by the players and public.

No better proof of which is an incident that occurred in the late 1930s. When it became known that the aforementioned Jack Hobbs was making his farewell appearance at the SCG, The Hill passed round a hat to get a present for this great batsman. At the conclusion of Hobbs's final innings, he walked round the ground, waving the boomerang that had been presented to him. Nearing the end of the circuit, he paused opposite The Hill, asking Yabba to come down to the fence.

Hobbs shook hands with Yabba and had a few words with him while thousands at the SCG cheered these two men who had, on opposite sides of the fence, done so much for the noble game of cricket.

Well after Yabba died, a letter to the *Herald* recounted, with great affection, some of his more immortal lines. The letter finished: 'Once he left the Sydney Cricket Ground, he (Yabba) was lost in oblivion, but when he appeared at his 'stand' in the middle of The Hill and among his thousands of subjects, he was King of all he surveyed.'

He was a good 'un all right—and he was one of ours.

The Greatest Cricket Team of All Time

WITH THE CONCLUSION of every cricket season, there is nothing surer than the bleeding endless selection of World XIs picked from all the players available. This is a journalistic cliché and a terrible bore to boot. Instead, let us select a team from the truly great players of history.

The openers: Could we do better than a pairing of the Good Samaritan and Paul Keating? In Sammy we would have a very solid, dependable type playing a selfless game with a totally straight bat. Perfect for the part. To complement him, Paul Keating has the capacity for hard work and just that necessary bit of mongrel in him that one of the openers must have. No mercy on the loose ball and unafraid to have a go if the risk is acceptable. I also believe he'd give a very good account of himself when it comes time to engage in a bit of light sledging, too. No reflection on Mr Keating, but Judas Iscariot would have been another serious contender as opener but for his unfortunate predilection for running his partners out, betraying them mid-pitch while he just looks after himself.

First drop: Winnie Churchill. When the darkest hour cometh, when one or both of the openers have been dismissed cheaply and the chips are down, you need a man with grit, with leadership, who will pay any price for victory and do anything to avoid defeat. If necessary, Winnie could hold up one end all day; or equally, if we started getting on top, the Great Man could belt fours and sixes to all parts of the ground.

Second drop and captain: Don Bradman. 'Nough said? No team selected from the ages would be complete if The Don was not a part of it, and, of course, he would also be captain.

Third drop: Charles de Gaulle. I know what you're thinking: you're thinking that the way Crazy Charlie plays his French cricket, with his bat just straight up and down in front of his pads, in front of his stumps, it will be hard for him to get runs and he'll also be very susceptible to LBW decisions. But that's where you're wrong. Not only is it devilishly hard for the bowlers to get Charlie out when he plays like that, but the guy can snick and deflect balls like you wouldn't believe. Sure, he's a pompous pain, and I can't wear him getting round saying, 'The team, *c'est moi*!', either, but we need him.

All-rounder: For the middle of the line-up, we need a rogue: A tearaway. A guy who likes riding roughshod wherever he goes. We need Ned Kelly. Not only would Ned do the job but he would refuse to be intimidated either by the opposition or the umpires, and I think he'd end up being a big crowd puller, too. Besides, with that big beard of his, he reminds one of the inimitable W.G. Grace.

Wicketkeeper: Chairman Mao. I dunno, he just looks the part. Sort of short and squat, like a wicketkeeper should. Plus, I reckon when it came to giving Prime Minister Keating a hand in the sledging department, the chairman could give them some of the choicer readings from his little red book until their noses bled.

Opening fast bowler: Sure, I am tempted by that kooky little tearaway German, Hitler, but, in the end, Adolf is too wild. In the end, six bouncers an over are just too much, and his respect for the rules is as non-existent as his decorum at after-match functions is abysmal. Besides which, when he plays, we may very well be no-balled out of the whole match. So, instead, let us go with Genghis Khan. Just the sight of Genghis tearing in from his long run-up with his hair trailing in the wind and that fearful glint in his eye as he screams imprecations into the wind would be enough to turn the strongest batsman's heart to water.

New-ball bowler: There'll be no relenting from the other end, either. Attila the Hun is the other opening bowler, for exactly the same reasons. Genghis and Attila—the ultimate opening bowlers. Who could withstand them?

Swing-bowler: Moses is the man. Moses can break opposition defences open as wide as the Red Sea, and he also does a very nice little line in miracles when the going is really tough—a crucial thing to have in one's corner for any cricket team. You might remember that time when South Africa needed twenty-three runs off the last ball to win against England. Somehow, I bet if Moses had been playing he would have managed it.

Spin-bowler: Someone devious, someone who knows all the tricks, but disguises it. A guy who looks as if he's bowling up lollipops when in fact they're cleverly disguised hand grenades. Someone who knows how to pick the lock of the opposition's defences without them having even the slightest clue of what is going on. Who else but Harry Houdini? Ambling up to the wicket, he would surely make the batsmen drool in expectation at the boundaries they were about to hit . . . Ol' Harry would give them thunder when they least expected it.

Twelfth man: Manuel from Fawlty Towers. No-one carries drinks as he does, and he may also be good for a bit of comic relief.

Finally, as *umpires* I should like a couple of nice, all-forgiving outstandingly human types like Florence Nightingale and Barry Manilow to be installed when the World is batting, and maybe we could at least give Hitler and Stalin a chance to participate as umpires when the Martians are at the crease.

A stand-by umpire, incidentally, when one or other of the uppity Martians refuses to walk, might be Oliver Cromwell: 'I implore you in the bowels of Christ, go, you are not wanted here.'

The Night Rugby's Holy Grail was Taken on a Bender

LAST NIGHT'S ABOMINABLE whisky was causing a wild African wail of hammering drums—*ka-thud thud-thud-thud, ka-thud thud-thud-thud*—to beat about two inches inside my left temple. Beside me, the famous English writer, Jeffrey Bernard, was being more than just a little unwell.

Behind us, following our weaving course, the police car was closing in. And between us, the bloody Rugby World Cup kept falling through the seats to knock my hand from the gear stick. No kidding, it was a bad day, a mean day, an ugly day, a 'shoot-me-before-I-go-mad' day.

How it all came to this I still don't quite know, so cloudy were the after-effects of the whisky. But after we'd pulled over and Jeffrey Bernard had been unwell on the pavement, after the police car had been persuaded to leave us alone, and after we'd finally got that hefty brute of a Bill Ellis Trophy fully upright again—in its carrying case and everything—I was at least able to start thinking partially straight again.

I suppose, for Australia, it all started on Nov 2 when the Queen gave Nick Farr-Jones the World Cup at Twickenham and rugby union's Holy Grail thus passed into Australia's hands . . . In the beginning, there was great ceremonial fanfare for the Cup as it was fêted throughout the great salons of the land. Photographed from all angles, toasted by the people and politicians alike, it was the symbol of our rugby supremacy and treated with extraordinary reverence by the whole population.

The high point of this reverence was undoubtedly when it was cheered by countless thousands as it travelled down Sydney's George Street in a full-blown ticker-tape parade. And from the glory of this, to being almost arrested in the company of Jeffrey Bernard and myself on the Sydney Harbour Bridge, I suppose must seem an extraordinary downward leap for the Cup. But you gotta understand . . .

Instead of confining the Cup to a gleaming glass case somewhere, the Australian Rugby Union took the attitude that if you're going to win such a proud flag of valour, the only sensible thing to do is to wave it around. Thus it started popping up everywhere—even in Hobart the previous Thursday night, when I went to speak there at a rugby dinner.

And what a hit the Cup was. In a typically wild, rollicking rugby evening, with mayhem breaking out everywhere, the local lads had a marvellous time with the Cup, knocked out that they could actually touch the code's most holy object.

But enough carousing and photographing . . . would I mind, my Tasmanian countrymen asked, taking the World Cup back to Sydney for them the following morning?

Not at all, not at all. Just as I hadn't minded when asked if I would like to take care of Jeffrey Bernard for a few days while he was in Sydney to promote the play about himself, *Jeffrey Bernard is Unwell.*

One thing led to another, and before you knew it, there we were . . . on the bridge, with the Cup, pursued by the cops.

Was it Jeffrey's state of health that moved the policemen on? Or perhaps even that he and I together, in moods as filthy as the ones we were in, mustn't have looked like the sort of people even a policeman should risk messing with. (If only they'd known that my companion was a convicted killer of rubber plants in an Indian restaurant.) Whatever, the cops eventually moved on and the Englishman and I were spared the task of explaining what such an unlikely pair of lads as ourselves were doing with such a gleaming trophy.

We were thus free to take the Cup to lunch, where, feeling better, the former rugby hooker, Jeffrey Bernard, pronounced himself happy that 'if England can't have the Cup, then at least it's good that the Australians have it . . . anybody but the wretched French and the bloody Welsh, who never bought a drink for anybody in their life'. Which accusation nobody could ever level at Jeffrey Bernard. It was a long lunch in the presence of our new-found friend, the Rugby World Cup.

Incidentally, be assured that for all its many travels, the Cup itself is in perfect shape without a single scratch upon it. There is only some slight damage to its carrying case, but that is to be expected.

Should England win the World Cup next time round, you will undoubtedly notice that a small shard of plexiglass is missing from the said carrying case. To recover this, you must go to the Coach and Horses pub in Soho, where you will find a drunken Jeffrey Bernard still confounding the dire predictions of all his doctors. Feel around in the top pocket of his blazer; there you will find the shard.

In the meantime, as Bernard says, 'England may not have the World Cup, but at least in my fair English blazer pocket there will always be a part of it.' Or something like that.

Your Mr Bernard is, by the by, even if unwell, a terrific fellow. If the police had not given us the benefit of the doubt, I should have been more than a little proud to go to gaol in his company, together with the Cup.

This way, though, it's easier. At least now England will not have to play an Australian prison side, led by Jeffrey Bernard and myself, to win the World Cup back in 1995.

Let's Win One for the Gipper

I LOVE THIS STORY.

It's the American 'win one for the Gipper' saga, from the second decade of the century . . .

George F. Gipp was the star running-back of the University of Notre Dame's gridiron team. A charismatic and naturally gifted player, Gipp's athletic abilities were only equalled by his passion for the nocturnal pleasures of playing pool and poker. Knute Rockne was his stern disciplinarian coach and Gipp was the only member of the team for whom Rockne would make allowances when it came to matters of discipline. So much so that when the slender Gipp was expelled from Notre Dame for failing in his grades, Rockne intervened on his behalf and had him reinstated.

Gipp showed his appreciation by blitzing 'em with even greater vigour than before—on one occasion in 1919 gaining 480 rushing yards for the fighting Irish against the Army side. A sportswriter of the time, George Trevor, wrote on that occasion that Gipp 'blazes fiercely like a meteor, not long destined to dazzle earthly eyes'.

The words were to prove prophetic for, as the winter of late 1919 set in, Gipp developed a persistent cough, perhaps exacerbated by his excessive smoking. Rockne considered Gipp too sick to play against the North-Western University side, but the crowd would have none of it and when they took up the chant of 'We want Gipp!', Rockne put him on to score two touchdowns on an afternoon cold enough to snap nose hairs with a sneeze.

The night after the game, Gipp's condition worsened. Hospital . . . prayers . . . last rites.

On the morning of 14 December 1919 coach Rockne was one of the last visitors to Gipp's bedside and the two spoke briefly.

When Gipp died, almost the entire student body accompanied his coffin to the local railway station. As the train made its way back to his hometown of Lanrium, Michigan, people lined the way to see 'the Gipper's train'. When they finally put him beneath the sod, a snowstorm like the people had never seen blew up from Lake Michigan.

Long years passed.

The scene now moves to 1928, to halftime of a game when Notre Dame are up against it as they play an Army side gone wild at Yankee Stadium.

Rockne, still coach, gathers his battered players around him and, at long last, divulges the contents of the conversation he'd had at Gipp's deathbed all those years ago. The players huddle in tight as Rockne's voice drops to an almost unearthly whisper.

'You see, boys, what the Gipper told me that night was this . . . "I've got to go, Rock. It's all right, I'm not afraid. Sometime, Rock, when the going isn't so easy, when the breaks are beating the boys, tell them to go in there with all they've got and to win a game for me—for the Gipper. I don't know where I'll be then, Rock, but I'll know about it, and I'll be happy."'

The upshot of the story, of course, is that the Notre Dame team were so moved by the words that they went back out

ent fields, all of which I've combed extensively over the last ten years or so looking for the best of the best. (You can call me 'a dedicated and selfless searcher for the Truth in all things' if you like, but that's just the way I am.)

But here goes . . .

Literature is the first field to explore, and of course it's hard to go past the activities of the Marquis de Sade and his writings, but what the hey?

For mine the truly best sexual horror story ever written was by the great writer, Roald Dahl, in his short story, *The Visitor*.

It's the story of a modern English Lothario driving through the Egyptian desert in the 1950s whose car breaks down, and ends up spending the night in the home of a rich local.

The man turns out to have a beautiful wife and an even more stunning daughter, and at the end of a wonderful evening of wining and dining, the Englishman is confident that his charms have worked their spell.

Sure enough, in the silent watch of the night, in the pitch black, a woman tip-toes to his bed, makes stupendous love to him for over four hours, and his only frustration is that through it all he is unable to discern whether it is the mother or the daughter—and she refuses to speak at all.

The following morning at breakfast the Englishman looks eagerly for signs, but apart from noticing with wonder that *both* women seem particularly gleeful, he is able to discern nothing out of the ordinary. After breakfast he leaves with the father of the house back to pick up his now-repaired car, and is still none the wiser.

It is during the drive that the father confides to him the reason he has taken his family to live out here in the desert. It's because he has another daughter, one who was in the house the previous night—but who he regrets the Englishman did not meet, just as she never met anyone who was not part of the immediate family.

'*But why?*' (the Englishman asks).

'*She has leprosy.*'

I jumped.

Calm yourself down! Mr Cornelius, calm yourself down! There's absolutely nothing in the world for you to worry about. It is not a very contagious disease. You have to have the most intimate *contact with the person in order to catch it . . .'*

A pause here, while we all shiver.

Gawd but I love that story. And in case you're trying to pick holes, note that in Dahl's story the girl did not suffer from the usual form of leprosy, which would have been easily determinable in the dark, when her elbow fell off, but a different strain which was just as ultimately damaging but entirely internal in its manifestation.

Anyway, moving right along. Another bit of sexual horror from literature which has always retained a certain *je-ne-sais-quoi* of horribleness long after I first heard it is:

A young man set sail from Bombay.
On a slow boat to China one day.
And got trapped near the tiller,
With a sex-crazed Gorilla.
And to China . . . it's a BLOODY long way.

Urban Myths are another promising field for sexual horror stories. They are the stories that always happened to a 'friend of a friend', which are recounted as being gospel truth but are always very light on for rock-solid details.

Like the story of the fellow with the incredibly large penis . . .

This was, of course, absolutely thuper for his self-esteem, but at least fate had evened things up a bit by also giving him a particularly low blood pressure. So the story goes, the combination created a particularly difficult problem for him, as it meant that every time he had an erection he would immediately faint dead away.

Sure enough, many doctors claim to have 'a friend of a friend', who they swear treated this man, but none claim to have actually treated him themselves.

From surely the same field of urban mythology comes the story of the bully at an exclusive boarding school in Sydney's eastern suburbs. As bullies go this fellow was the absolute champeen champion, and something of a palace coup was eventually decided upon by the other boarders. Tired of being eternally pushed around, they conceived a plan based on the knowledge that the bully masturbated every night straight after 'lights out'.

The plan? Simply to mix several tubes of super-glue in the vaseline bottle, which the bully kept in his bedside drawer and used for his lubricant. Then, as soon as they heard the familiar *creak, creak, creak*, coming from his bed, one of the lads turned the lights on, of course forcing the fellow to freeze in his tracks, gripping himself tightly . . .

It was not a particularly simple matter for a surgeon to separate the two sets of skin, but he was immeasurably helped by the fact that all the blood that had been powering the lad's erection was now powering his progressively redder face.

The animal kingdom is often featured in urban myths and a story circulated late last year, for example, of a case in Western Australia where a judge is supposed to have ruled that no less than 500 dollars compensation was to be paid by the owners of a Chihuahua to the owners of a pedigreed Great Dane. It was claimed, and supposedly proven that the Chihuahua had impregnated the Great Dane.

You're right, it defies belief, and frankly I don't believe it.

News Items, on the other hand, have documented even stranger things happening with dogs. Like the absolutely shocking case that really did happen in England and emerged in court in February of this year . . .

It wasn't just what this fellow by the name of Derek Jeffrey, 59, liked to do with dogs that was the most horrible part, it was *how* the world found out about it.

In May of 1992, Mr Jeffrey had the misfortune to discover something of a passion for his neighbours' bull terrier, 'Ronnie', and liked to lure it to his bedroom where he could have his wicked way with it.

After several weeks of this practice though, he was still not satisfied that he had entirely explored the erotic potential of the whole thing and decided to record it all on his home video and be able to play it back at will. (*I know, I know, already this guy is not sounding like Einstein's little brother, right?*) Then his *real* mistake. Mr Jeffrey lent his camcorder to a friend with the video still in it, under the mistaken impression that the footage had been erased.

Along came the big day and at the wedding reception (*you're way ahead of me, right?*) somebody thought it would be a wonderful idea to have a look at the footage already shot of the wedding ceremony.

They got a television, pressed the 'play' button and there, in front of assembled guests, in full living colour were Mr Jeffrey and Ronnie, *en flagrante,* as it were. This of course was not the sort of thing you see with every man and his dog, and the guests were so shocked they informed the authorities. Mr Jeffrey was soon afterwards hauled before a judge and jury, who after witnessing the video 'remanded him on bail for psychiatric and other reports'. (What I want to know is what the neighbour said when he handed back the camcorder to Mr Jeffrey: 'listen, there's been a bit of a hitch . . .')

Medical Journals, though, can be a great source for your way above-average sexual horror stories. The best I ever came across was in the December '92 issue of Britain's *Sexual and Marital Therapy* journal, as reported in the *Independent* newspaper. It concerned the story of a man the journal referred to only as 'George'.

George was a 20 year old from a Midlands working-class family, who also had the distinction of belonging to a very repressive and strict religious sect. George's problem, and I'm not making this up, was that he had formed a bizarre erotic relationship with the family's Austin Metro. (And please spare me all obvious jokes about 'auto-eroticism' as they are simply too obvious to be funny.)

But anyway, the story is true.

Apparently, as a naturally shy boy whose sexual feelings for more normal things were wiped out by his parents' strong disapproval, the first thing that came into George's orbit that he could safely love was the family car.

Not knowing quite why it all excited him so, but perhaps

happy for the first time nevertheless, he began to masturbate when alone inside the car. And if he *really* wanted to get intimate, he would crouch down and sniff the fumes from the exhaust pipe when the engine was running.

This was particularly difficult of course when he didn't have his own licence, but as soon as he acquired it, he was away. George took the car to deserted car parks, quiet back-streets, and any other places he could find where he could be alone with the object of his desire.

Apparently he was quite monogamous, and though he would occasionally look sideways at the Vauxhall Nova, Vauxhall Astra, Fiat Uno and Ford Fiesta, all of whom resembled the Metro, he never went so far as to actually do anything with the other cars.

While the rest of us, of course, can scratch our heads in wonder at how George could get so sexually obsessed with a car (*apart from you Porsche owners I mean, who are no doubt wondering what the big deal is*), George apparently didn't think of it as a car.

He told his therapists, Padmal de Silva and Amanda Pernet at the Institute of Psychiatry, London, that for him the front of the Metro resembled a smiling child-like face. He also said that while he found the rear of the car quite unpleasant, it was nevertheless the most arousing to him, even though he was afraid of being polluted by exhaust fumes.

One should never be surprised at the bizarreness of people's *sexual peccadillos* of course (*I mean, we're all adults here, right?*) but sometimes it really does all but defy belief.

In the United States, Abigail Van Buren of 'Dear Abby' fame once released a list of the ten most peculiar letters she'd ever received and top of the pops was the story of an *extremely upset* new bride who had written to Abby from her honeymoon hotel. What do you do, Abby, she wanted to know, when your husband is a mortician and on your wedding night he confides that the only way he can have sex is with women who if they are not dead, at least pretend to be? What do you tell him when he wants you to lie in a cold bath for twenty minutes and then lie very, very still?

Regrettably Abby did not release her reply to this problem,

but I know what my reply would have revolved around. One word:

'TAXI!!!'

Speaking of weird though, try this single quote, giving a glimpse of a sexual world which most of us cannot even imagine:

'I drink only my own blood now. Drinking someone else's blood is better, of course, but I'm a safe sex vampire.' Jack, a 37-year-old gay vampire who lives in San Francisco, quoted in an *Advocate* story, 'Love in Vein; Inside the World of Gay Vampires'.

It is of course the sudden *public discovery* of such private sexual things which makes for true embarrassment. In this field it is hard to go past the case of the famed English literarist, Sir Edmund Gosse who was discovered in Westminster Abbey, during the funeral of no less a personage than Robert Browning, drooling over pictures of male nudes.

There but for the grace of God go us all, no? On lesser charges perhaps, but Somerset Maugham once said that 'there is not one of us who if all the ins and outs of our sexual lives were put on public display would not be thought of as monsters' and I for one think it's pretty true. At least for most of you.

But moving right along . . .

Sports, and most particularly, sportsmen, is another fertile area in which to look for shocking sex stories—perhaps because sportsmen, for some obscurely base reason (*sniff*), delight in telling them.

Anyway, as it happens, there are *two* sexual horror stories currently circulating about a couple of well-known footballers. It is hard to figure if they are actually true or not, as we have to ask ourselves if things really were this bad then how come we're hearing about them, but for what it's worth here they are . . .

After two long months of touring with the national side in Britain, a footballer is purported to have returned from the long and arduous trip to finally get back to bed with his wife.

While overseas he hasn't been particularly faithful, though he has at least been careful not to get himself attached to any one woman, and has in fact been mostly with married women, the better to ensure there are no problems with extrication.

Anyway, so the story goes, on the first night he is very careful to make particularly passionate love to his wife in the manner of one who has gone without for 8 weeks, and then falls into the sleep of the dead and the seriously jet-lagged.

As the first grey streaks of dawn enter the room he awakes with a start and, momentarily disoriented, manages to blurt out, 'oh my God, I've got to get out of here before your husband gets home!'

That's OK darlin',' she replies dreamily, 'he's over in England playing football.'

Boom. Boom.

The other is of a football star who, apparently, was making love so passionately to one particular girl, that right in the very throes of passion, bouncing up and down, *up* and *down*, UP and DOWN, he suddenly bounced right off and landed on the wood floor, bursting his engorged penis.

Twenty-seven stitches later he was basically OK, and you're right, it seems dubious to me too whether it actually happened, and I for one am not going to ask him, but such cases are not without precedent in the world of medicine.

It all gets weirder by the day.

If The Sun Goes Out

IF THE SUN WAS connected to a switch and in a fit of pique some wretch got his evil fingers on it to flick it off forever—let's say at 5p.m. this afternoon—what would happen over the next few hours, days, months and decades?

Tick, tick, tick, tick.

Nothing at all for eight minutes, as that's how long it takes light to travel from the sun to our own fair planet, sunnyside up. Then, as the last rays hit, it would be like a light suddenly going out, as the air gradually cooled and the birds, fooled into thinking that night had fallen, would go quiet as they bedded down for the early evening.

Then for the span of several hours there would be little difference from a normal night except that without the sun there would be no moon visible. A few planetary observers on the dark side of the planet would notice Venus suddenly flickering off and then, one by one, all the other planets too would disappear.

The only source of night light would then be from the distant stars and without the light of the moon to compete with, they would be bright as never before. Falling meteorites would come up a treat. But then as the long darkness continued with still no return of solar warmth, the entire planet would continue to gradually cool. The only source of natural warmth for the earth would be its interior and that would not be nearly hot enough to keep the surface warm.

It would be very still. Winds, which are caused by unevenness in the temperature of the earth's surface, would gradually calm and after a period of probably three or four days would cease almost entirely. The tides would continue unaffected but the waves of the ocean, which are almost entirely wind-driven, would gradually diminish. After a week, a person walking along Bondi Beach holding up a flaming torch would surely remark on the eery stillness of the ocean. There would be no more crashing of the breakers on the shore, just a gentle gurgle as the mighty Pacific turned into a mill-pond.

It would take a long time yet for the oceans to fully freeze over, as they would retain enormous reserves of thermal energy. As a result, it is likely that of all living creatures, deep-sea fish would be the last to notice that things had gone awry.

How long human life could survive is a moot point. It would depend of course how well we could organise ourselves. But right from the beginning of the long night, plant life would begin to die as it was denied photo-synthesis. Such delicate planet life as flowers would wither almost immediately, grass would start to turn brown beneath the enveloping blackness, and while it would not be obvious, the hardier trees would also begin to die immediately.

For us humans to eat there would still be animal life of course—the cows and sheep not being so directly dependent on sunlight to live—and barring the cold, animals would continue to survive for some time, so long as they themselves had food. But the supply of plant life for the herbivorous animals to eat would now be an unreplenishable resource and every gram of grass eaten by a cow would bring them closer to their own extinction. Presently, they too would die.

With the earth converted into a massive cool room, the

best chance for longest survival would be to be in that part of the cool room which has preserved fruit in it. The closest of these to Sydney would probably be an hour to the north by car, in the orchards around Peat's Ridge. But soon, that supply of food too would run out.

Everywhere, all is quiet now. Those of us who had survived long enough for the air temperature to fall below freezing would be, for the most part, preserved pristine where we fell.

Beatrice Helen FitzSimons

O.A.M. (1920-1994)

AND NOW MUM has died, too. Yesterday. They took her out between the palm trees that mark the entrance to our farm, just like they did two years ago with Dad. This time in a white van. Can't believe it. Two months, from diagnosis to death.

Two months. Cancer. Jesus.

And they always say that in the last moments of people's lives they have this kind of video playing on fast-forward in their heads, with highlights of their life whisking past until the curtain comes down for keeps.

Maybe Mum did, maybe she didn't. But gathered around her death-bed at home on the farm, all six of us kids had our own Mum videos going flat out. Not 'highlights' exactly, but just things that stick in your memory, from our beginnings to her end.

I don't know, maybe it's not all actual memory, because I can remember things from long before I was actually born, but the visions of Mum's life just kept coming.

Mum, playing as a little girl, with her sister and friend at her Wahroonga home on Sydney's North Shore. Playing endlessly in the warm summer sun, in the intricately designed garden that her father built. She wrote some of her own poetry on this a long time later, encapsulating something of the feel of the time:

> We three, enjoyed our lives enormously,
> Playing cards and playing shops,
> With broken biscuits, making swaps.
> A minimum of household chores,
> Long days playing out of doors . . .
> > Hot days underneath the hose,
> There were no finer times than those.

A boat somewhere—Lake Louise in the Canadian Rockies, I think—and Mum as a young woman was out there on it, rocking gently back and forth. Enjoying a break from the frenetic pace of the world tour she was on with Grandpa and my Aunty Mary. She was reading a letter, from the fellow who had grown up only a few streets away, Peter McCloy FitzSimons, the same fellow she had been seeing a great deal of since the war they'd both returned safely from. He wrote of his overwhelming desire to marry her . . .

'On a good day,' Mum would tell us, 'your father would break a pick-handle before breakfast.'

True. It wasn't a great bit of land they'd got, but it was *their* land, their 'own dung-heap' as Dad called it, up the end of a winding dirt track at Peat's Ridge. They called the place 'Windhill'. And sure it was rocky, sure it took a hell of a lot of work from both of them to make the land produce agriculturally; but they were young, they had boundless energy, they had each other, they had no choice. If these two city kids gone bush were going to survive, extremely hard work was the only way.

One day, very early on, Aunty Dorothy—who was my grandfather's elderly sister and a very imposing North Shore lady to boot—came on a visit from the Big Smoke of Sydney, came to the primitive two-room shack Mum and Dad called home.

Aunty Dorothy was, by all reports, not too happy to find that not only was there no toilet inside, there was no toilet even *outside*. Unless you want to call a rough sort of latrine, out the back by the big pine tree, a toilet.

But, Mum, how did you cope? How did you manage such a marked change in lifestyle, going from a Wahroonga mansion with a live-in maid and gardener, to a two-room shack in the country without even the most basic of all basic facilities?

'I would have lived with your father in a *cave*,' was always Mum's firm reply.

And she meant it, too. After that first cheque for the first tomato crop came in, they were so happy that Mum and Dad's preferred phrase of the time was 'we wouldn't call the King our uncle!'

When she'd brought her fourth child home from the hospital, it had all seemed somewhat overwhelming. With Dad out on the farm all day long and David, Martin and Andrew scurrying around underfoot and little Cathy needing her nappy changed while the clothes needing a' washing, the stove a' stoking, the clothes a' mending, while the breakfast plates were still in the sink with Dad soon coming back for lunch and little Andrew crying again . . . it had looked impossible.

But she looked over and felt a sudden surge of optimism.

There was six-year-old David, holding a book and reading something out to three-year-old Andrew and the little one was listening, *laughing*.

So it went. The older ones taking progressively more care of the younger ones while more kids just kept on coming. Jum, Trish and then me.

Martin died. Mum cried. Endlessly.

As a two-year-old I was looking out, from beneath Mum's pink petticoats. She was standing in Mrs Slade's gardens chatting to her, and I had my head up beneath her petticoat, and now out again, and now back beneath her petticoat, watching each time how the sun would come through the pinkness of it and make everything around seem so cosy.

I was maybe ten years old, in a Holden station wagon chocka block with oranges and kids at the traffic lights at Pymble, heading south. Mum was sitting there in the driver's seat, playing her usual spelling games with us kids, when some young hoons pulled up in the lane beside us. In a kind of FJ Holden I guess they were. The driver kept revving the engine, rocking back and forth like he had pole position at Bathurst, just like he could barely *wait* for the light to turn green.

'And Petey-boy, how do you spell carrot?' Mum asked me over the revving engine, ignoring the hoons entirely though not taking her eyes off the traffic lights for a moment.

I don't know, maybe the guys in the FJ Holden had the misfortune to be rocking backwards when the green light hit, or maybe our station-wagon really was a pretty powerful beast for all its 'square' appearance.

All I know is that I was up to the first 'r' in carrot when Mum took her foot off the clutch, stamped the accelerator hard and we left the brutes standing—furiously spinning their wheels as they tried to make good lost ground.

My Mum *buried* 'em—all without turning a hair, or interrupting the spelling game for a second. As soon as the 'G' Force released me from being pinned to the back of the seat, I finished spelling carrot.

'The Lord looks after drunks, fools, and my wife,' Dad would always say, and on a round view of things, he was probably quite correct. Like hitch-hikers for example. As a breed they can be a fairly dangerous bunch, at least the male of the species, myself excepted, and women drivers on their own rightly steer clear of picking them up.

Not Mum.

No matter the time of night or day, she would always pick hitch-hikers up and take them as far as she could on their appointed course. If the night was dark, the weather foul, and their prospects ordinary, she would sometimes bring them back to the farm and persuade Dad to give them a few day's work.

One such fellow, by the name of Fred, an Eastern European who had been wandering the highways and byways of Australia for about forty years as near as we could reckon, came to stay for about three months in our shed. Crazy as a coot, and Dad wasn't actually that happy about it, but Mum worried about what might happen to him if he wasn't semi-taken care of—so he stayed till he was quite ready to drift away again . . .

'But Mum!' I exploded as a firebrand fourteen-year-old. 'Of *course* capital punishment has got to be justifiable in some cases! What if, just say, I came across Hitler and I knew he'd killed six million Jews and I had a gun. What would you have me do?'

'Tie a rope around his leg.'

In forty-four years of marriage, Dad had never had to do it before, but enough was enough. It was time for real rebellion.

'I can't eat this,' he said, pushing the plate away from him. The source of his distaste? It wasn't just that it was left-over salad, for Dad could have handled that. Not even that it was *two weeks old* salad, for again, at a pinch Dad could just maybe have managed to cope with eating that, too. It was, precisely, that in Mum's last ditch effort to do anything rather than throw food out, she had BOILED this salad, then served it up as a kind of hot meal.

Dad had finally found his limits, but Mum refused to accept defeat and kept eating. Helen FitzSimons, frugal be thy name.

It was at a ceremony up at Mangrove Mountain, to mark Mum having been awarded the Order of Australia for community service. One after the other these people that most of the rest of the family had never seen got up to bear testimony to Mum's deep involvement with their organisations: the Country Women's Association, Garden Club, P & C, Brownies, Community Hall, Community Newspaper, Scouts, Guides, Cubs and on and on into the ever etcetera . . .

So *that* was where Mum had been all these years. No kidding, the refrain of my youth was one question and one answer.

'Where's Mum?'

'Up the Ridge.'

Up the Ridge. If she wasn't 'down the patch' with Dad, or in the house with the family, Mum was always up the ridge doing something with one community organisation or other. Ever and always.

Mum, on the couch, telling my son Jake the same poems she'd told me when I was a wee one. Telling him my favourite poem of all, with all the appropriate facial expressions and emphasis on particular words:

> *There was a little birdy,*
> *Sitting in a tree,*
> *Singing just as happily as can be . . .*
> *When along came a* MAN,
> *With a great big* GUN,
> *And he* SHOT *that little birdie,*
> JUST FOR FUN.
>
> *I'd rather be a* RAT,
> *Or the worst kind of* CAT,
> *Than a* MAN *with a* GUN,
> *Who would shoot a little birdie,*
> JUST FOR FUN . . .

Jake gurgles away, and keeps trying to interrupt Grandma by putting his fist in her mouth and dribbling on her nightie. He doesn't understand the words now, but he will.

A small walk, soon after Mum came home from the operation, just a month ago. Back along the track that led from the new house back to the old cottage they'd started out in. Could it be that, weak as she was, for one time in her life Mum would be able to walk two hundred metres without picking every weed she saw as well as picking up every stray bit of paper? No chance. I, too, was conscripted to pick up every one, whingeing about it all the way, just like I used to.

And now we are back in the here and now, and Mum's body is

still warm on the bed before us—her six children, our spouses and assorted grandchildren. At the end of this truly beautiful July day, amazingly warm in the middle of winter, the red light of sunset is streaming into her room.

We are, all of us, family in this room, family in a linked circle around Mum, holding each other.

And I don't know if it was Trish or Jum started singing it first, but one of them started singing the words of the hymn *Jerusalem* and we all join in:

And did those feet in ancient times,
Walk upon England's mountain green?
And was the holy lamb of God
On England's pleasant pastures seen?

A couple of days previously, Mum had roused herself from her death-bed when we were having a sing-along to tell me that I was so badly out of tune that she'd really rather I stopped, but this was no time to think of that. We all belted it out as one, till we were done . . .

Bring me my bow of burning gold
Bring me my arrows of desire
Bring my spears, oh hearts unfold,
Bring me chariots of fire.

A traffic jam, a real live traffic jam, came on the old road leading into the farm, about ten minutes before Mum's memorial service on the lawns of Windhill was about to start. Three hundred people strong. Everyone would like to think they'd get a traffic jam at their funeral. My Mum really got one.

I am proud to be her son.